SHELTERBELTS

SHELTERBELTS

JONATHAN DYCK

SHELTERBELTS

FIRST EDITION
PRINTED BY GAUVIN IN QUEBEC, CANADA

LIBRARY AND ARCHIVES CANADA CATALOGUING IN PUBLICATION
TITLE: SHELTERBELTS / JONATHAN DYCK.
NAMES: DYCK, JONATHAN, AUTHOR, ARTIST.
IDENTIFIERS: CANADIANA 2022014737X | ISBN 9781772620689 (SOFTCOVER)
SUBJECTS: LCGFT: GRAPHIC NOVELS.
CLASSIFICATION: LCC PN6733.D93 S54 2022 | DDC 741.5/971 — dc23

CONUNDRUM PRESS
WOLFVILLE, NS, CANADA
WWW.CONUNDRUMPRESS.COM

CONUNDRUM PRESS ACKNOWLEDGES THE FINANCIAL SUPPORT OF THE CANADA COUNCIL FOR THE ARTS, THE GOVERNMENT OF CANADA, AND THE PROVINCE OF NOVA SCOTIA TOWARD OUR PUBLISHING PROGRAM.

CONUNDRUM PRESS IS LOCATED IN MI'KMA'KI, THE ANCESTRAL AND UNCEDED TERRITORY OF THE MI'KMAQ PEOPLE.

Canada Council for the Arts Conseil des Arts du Canada

THE AUTHOR GRATEFULLY ACKNOWLEDGES FINANCIAL ASSISTANCE PROVIDED BY THE MANITOBA ARTS COUNCIL.

"LIFE IS NOT A WALK ACROSS AN OPEN FIELD."
— RUSSIAN PROVERB

MAIN CHARACTERS IN ORDER OF APPEARANCE

SUSIE TEICHROBE
FRIEND TO JESS AND REBECCA

JESS SUDERMAN
DAUGHTER TO PASTOR GERHARD, FRIEND TO SUSIE AND REBECCA

MIKE WALL
PASTOR OF PARK VALLEY CHURCH

GERHARD SUDERMAN
PASTOR OF JUBILEE MENNONITE CHURCH (JMC), FATHER TO JESS

CATHY NEUFELD
FORMER MEMBER OF JMC, WIFE TO HENRY

JUDITH SAWATZKY
HIGH SCHOOL ENGLISH TEACHER, FRIEND TO PETE

PETE DAVIS
HIGH SCHOOL HISTORY TEACHER, FRIEND TO GERHARD AND JUDITH

KAREN PETERS
LIBRARIAN, MEMBER OF JMC, MOTHER TO REBECCA

HENRY NEUFELD
FORMER MEMBER OF JMC, HUSBAND TO CATHY

REBECCA PETERS
DAUGHTER TO KAREN, PARTNER TO JASON

CINDY PENNER
WIFE TO BILL, FRIEND TO DEB

BILL PENNER
FARMER, HUSBAND TO CINDY

JASON MORRISSEAU
BIKE MECHANIC, PARTNER TO REBECCA, FRIEND TO JESS

THOMAS REIMER
SON TO DEB AND ABE ATTENDS PARK VALLEY

DEB REIMER
MOTHER TO THOMAS, WIFE TO ABE, MEMBER OF BIBLE MENNONITE FELLOWSHIP (BMF)

IKE FRIESEN
FARMER, BROTHER TO JEN

JEN FRIESEN
FARMER, SISTER TO IKE

LARISSA GOERTZEN
PARTNER TO DEREK, ATTENDS PARK VALLEY

DEREK DRIEDGER
PARTNER TO LARISSA, COUSIN TO REBECCA GREW UP ATTENDING JMC

ALF SIEMENS
LOCAL HISTORIAN, MEMBER OF BMF

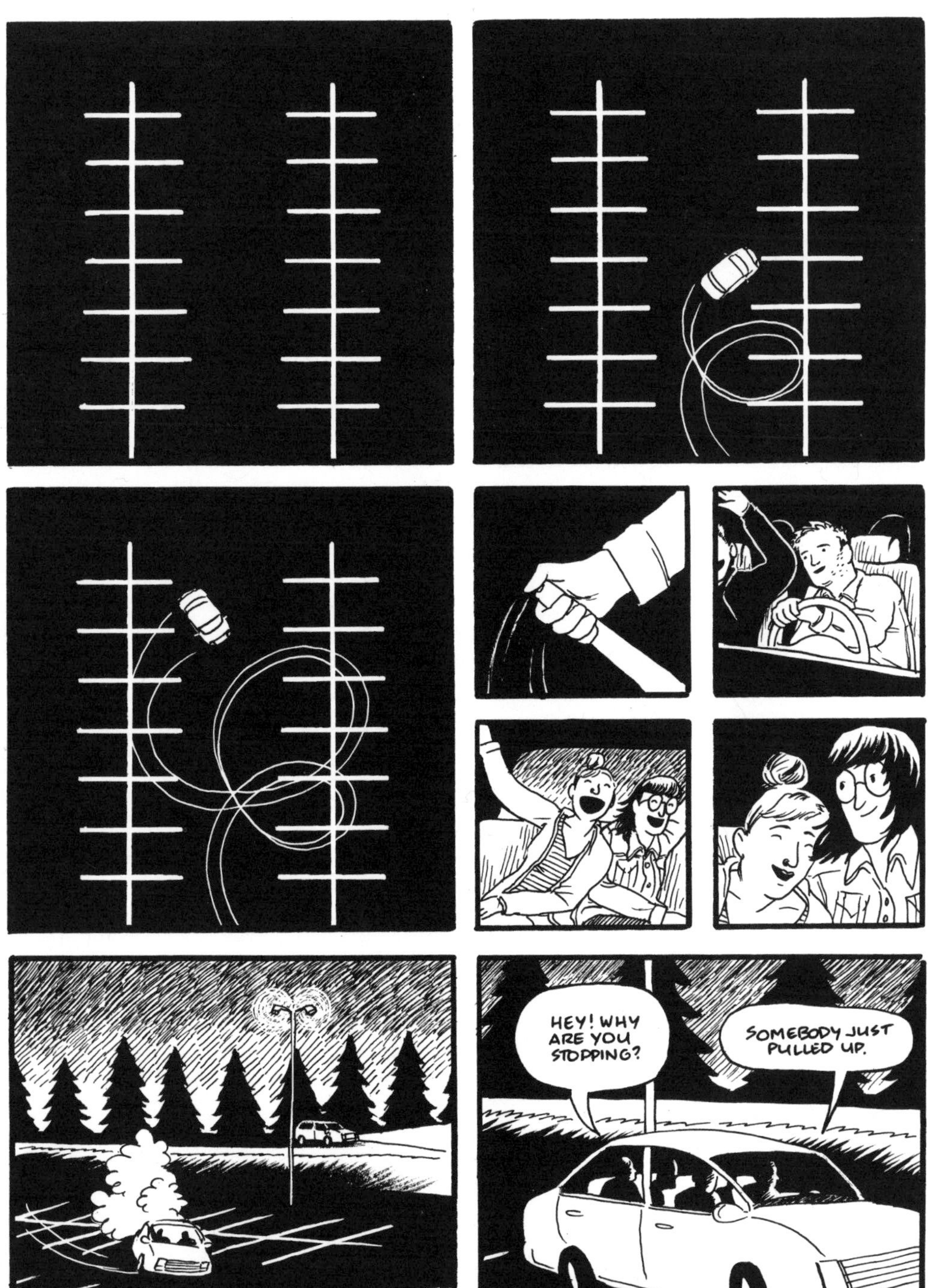
HEY! WHY ARE YOU STOPPING?
SOMEBODY JUST PULLED UP.

AW, MAN. I GUESS WE SHOULD GET OUTTA HERE.

VALLEY
RCH
VICES
PM • 6 PM
PARK VALLEY CHURCH

LEY CHURCH

UGH. I HATE THAT PLACE.
HEY SUSIE, DO YOU HAVE ANY ROAD POPS LEFT?

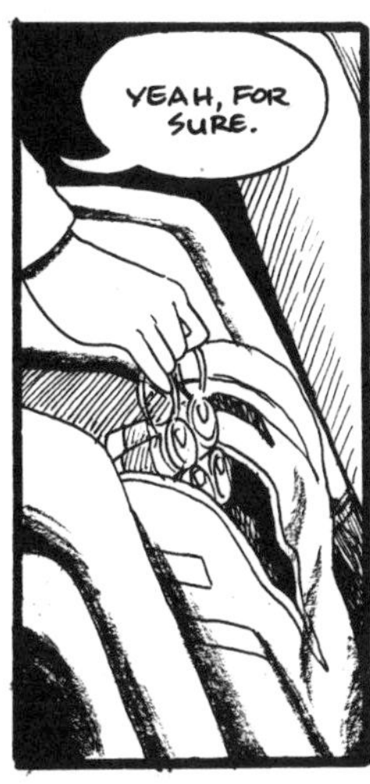
YEAH, FOR SURE.

CAN YOU GUYS AT LEAST WAIT 'TIL WE'RE ON A COUNTRY ROAD?

BUZZ

8:15
Marley
Don't stay too late. You promised the girls you'd read them some Narnia before bed tonight.

Kind of stuck tbh.
Well, it never hurts to pray about it. ☺ Just write the sermon you needed to hear before you met me. ♡♡♡♡
you got this, babe. XO

THE MESSAGE
CONCORDANCE
NEW TESTAMENT

PARK VALLEY CHURCH
SERVICES:
10 AM · 2 PM · 6 PM

YAWN

SOMEONE LEFT THIS BREAD ON THE PORCH.

OH, THAT MUST BE FROM KAREN AT CHURCH -REBECCA'S MOM.

I KNOW WHO KAREN IS, DAD. THAT WOMAN IS SO FRIGGIN' NICE.

I WAS JUST THINKING ABOUT TAKING A BREAK. WANNA PLAY SOME DARTS?
YOU'RE STILL NOT DONE YOUR SERMON?
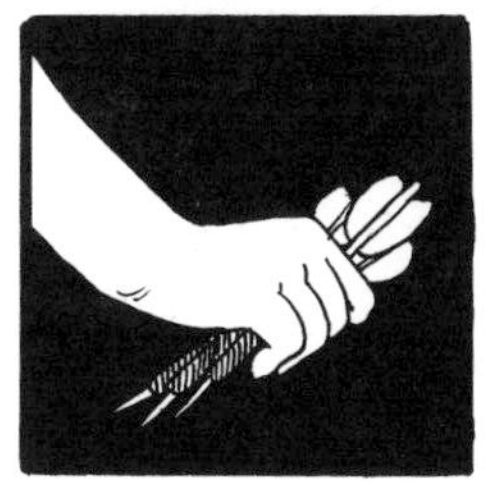

... SO WHAT ARE YOU PREACHING ON TOMORROW?
WELL, THE TEXT IS FROM 1 PETER, SO I WAS THINKING...

I'M GOING TO SPEAK ABOUT BEING CALLED OUT.

YOU GOT CALLED OUT?

OH, HEHE-NO, NOT IN THAT SENSE. THE GREEK WORD USED FOR THE EARLY CHURCH-EKKLESIA-IT LITERALLY MEANS THOSE WHO ARE CALLED OUT.
AS IN, CALLED OUT OF DARKNESS AND INTO LIGHT.
RIGHT.

WE TEND TO FOCUS ON WHAT WE'RE BEING CALLED OUT OF...

BUT IT'S REALLY ABOUT WHAT WE'RE BEING CALLED INTO.
I FEEL LIKE I'VE HEARD THIS ONE BEFORE.

COMING TOMORROW?
WE'LL SEE. 'NIGHT DAD.

TRUTH

ONE OF THE GREAT MYTHS OF THE MODERN AGE IS THAT WE ARE IN CONTROL OF OUR OWN LIVES.

BUT DEEP DOWN EVERY-ONE KNOWS THE TRUTH: WE'RE ALL TRAPPED.

YOU CAN SEE IT ALL AROUND YOU: PEOPLE TRYING TO ESCAPE THIS REALITY WITH DRUGS, AND ALCOHOL, PROMISCUITY AND SEXUAL EXPERIMENTATION. THE LIST GOES ON AND ON.
ISAIAH 12:
PARK VALLE

MAYBE IT'S THAT BRAND NEW TRUCK YOU'VE BEEN SAVING FOR, OR THAT PROMOTION AT WORK, OR THAT FAMILY VACATION AT DISNEY WORLD.

BUT YOU AND I KNOW THAT NONE OF THESE THINGS — NOTHING IN THIS WORLD — WILL FREE US.

ONLY GOD HAS THE POWER TO DO THAT! AND HE DID! BY SENDING HIS SON, JESUS.

EVERY BLESSING, EVERY TEMPTATION IS AN INVITATION FROM GOD TO GROW CLOSER TO HIM.

MY WIFE, OUR KIDS, THIS WONDERFUL COMMUNITY – THE BEST PARTS OF MY LIFE CAME WHEN I CHOSE TO FOLLOW HIS WILL AND NOT MY OWN.

JUBILEE MENNONITE
CHURCH

NIRV

PRINCE
· OF ·
PEACE

KING OF KINGS
PRINCE OF PEACE

Romans

HEY DAD, MY SHIFT ENDED EARLY SO I WENT FOR A WALK NEARBY.

I'M AT THE CORNER OF SPRUCE AND POPLAR AVE. NO RUSH.

I MEAN, IT'S RESIDENTIAL, AND IT'S A WEEKNIGHT, AND THERE'S LITERALLY NO ONE OUTSIDE RIGHT NOW.

HEY!

WELL IT LOOKS LIKE OUR CHURCH JUST LOST ANOTHER FAMILY.

IT WAS OVER THE LGBTQ ISSUE.

SORRY, I KNOW ISSUE ISN'T THE RIGHT WORD.

DID THEY, UM, SPEAK TO YOU DIRECTLY ABOUT IT?

THEY TALKED TO SEVERAL PEOPLE WHO ALL SUGGESTED THEY TALK TO ME.

THERE WAS A VISIONING MEETING A FEW WEEKS AGO WHERE SOMEONE SAID WE SHOULD THINK ABOUT BEING MORE EXPLICIT IN OUR LANGUAGE.

MORE WELCOMING TO PEOPLE LIKE...
LIKE YOUR GAY DAUGHTER?
HAHA. YES.

AND THEN THERE WAS THAT HYMN WE SANG ON SUNDAY.

OH YEAH! THE ONE WITH THE LINE ABOUT LOVING ALL GENDERS...

AND THE VERY OBVIOUS RAINBOW METAPHOR.
YEAH.

CATHY- MRS. NEUFELD-CALLED THIS AFTERNOON TO LET ME KNOW.

SHE WAS IN MY OFFICE EARLIER THIS WEEK AND THINGS GOT... A BIT HEATED. I SUPPOSE IT WAS HER LAST RESORT.

SHE SAID SHE'S CERTAIN ABOUT WHERE SHE STANDS ON THE ISSUE AND JUST AS CERTAIN ABOUT WHAT THE BIBLE SAYS.

I'M GUESSING IT'S THE ONLY BOOK SHE'S EVER READ.
WELL, IT'S AN OPINION SHE'S HELD FOR A LONG TIME.

I TOLD HER THAT WE HAVE A SPECTRUM OF VIEWS AT THE CHURCH.

5:36
Susie
K. Let's do it tomorrow. Sorry I had to cancel! Can't wait to catch uppp!!! xoxo

BUT WE'VE AGREED THAT WE CAN ALL STILL WORSHIP TOGETHER, THAT THERE'S ENOUGH COMMON GROUND ELSEWHERE.

AT THE END OF THE DAY I'M STILL THEIR PASTOR, AND I HAVE TO BALANCE THAT WITH MY OWN PERSONAL VIEWS.

SOUNDS LIKE YOU'VE ALREADY DECIDED THAT YOU'RE GIVING UP.

YOU DON'T NEED TO DEVELOP IT ALL AT ONCE, ESPECIALLY AS MORE OF THIS FARMLAND TURNS COMMERCIAL... THE VALUE WILL JUST KEEP CLIMBING.
PARK

THE NEW SKATEPARK IS OUR FIRST PRIORITY, BUT WE'VE ALSO BEEN DREAMING ABOUT USING THIS AREA FOR A COFFEE SHOP AND POTENTIAL BUSINESS PARTNERSHIPS.

WELL, THE LAND'S NOT CHEAP AND THOSE TREES WILL NEED TO GO IF YOU WANT DIRECT ACCESS TO THE HIGHWAY.
TAP
TAP

I'LL BE MEETING WITH THE REST OF THE PASTORAL TEAM TO TALK FUNDING STRATEGY BUT WE DON'T WANT TO RUSH INTO ANYTHING.

THANKS TO YOU, THE CHURCH IS REALLY GROWING—I THINK GOD IS TRYING TO TELL US SOMETHING. THIS MIGHT BE THE RIGHT TIME TO EXPAND.

IF WE AREN'T GROWING, WE'RE STAGNATING... BUT IT'S NOT JUST ABOUT NUMBERS. IT'S ALSO SPIRITUAL.
ALL I'M SAYING IS YOU'LL NEED TO ACT FAST IF YOU'RE SERIOUS ABOUT IT.

WE'LL TAKE SOME TIME TO DISCERN AND PRAY. SEE YOU SUNDAY!

SCREECH!

GODDAMN WHITE TAILS!

YOU'RE NOT EVEN SUPPOSED TO BE HERE!

GAS

HEY JAKE..., YEAH, PLEASE GO AHEAD AND START ON THE PAPERWORK. I'M SURE I'LL BE ABLE TO BRING EVERYONE ON BOARD.

THERE'S NO TIME TO WASTE WHEN IT COMES TO OUTREACH. GOD IS GIVING US THIS OPPORTUNITY TO EXPAND FOR A REASON.

OP
ROCERY

SO YOU GUYS WANNA CRUISE AROUND AGAIN TONIGHT?
I HEARD THERE'S GONNA BE A FIRE DOWN AT THE GRAVEL PITS.

I'M WORKING AT THE GAS BAR TONIGHT, SO MAYBE AFTER? I CAN PICK YOU UP.

THAT SOUNDS A BIT TOO LATE FOR ME.

WHAT—YOU'VE GOTTA BE UP FOR CHURCH OR SOME THING TOMORROW?

HAH, YEAH RIGHT...

IT WOULD SUCK TO BE A PASTOR'S KID.
AT LEAST IT'S NOT AT ONE OF THOSE REALLY CONSERVATIVE CHURCHES.
LIKE, WHERE THE WOMEN AREN'T ALLOWED TO SPEAK.

I LIKE YOUR DAD. SEEMS LIKE AN OKAY GUY.
YEAH, HE TRIES TO BE, I GUESS.
FLICK

HEY, DON'T YOUR PARENTS GO TO ONE OF THOSE CHURCHES?
SHUT UP.
I BETTER GET BACK TO WORK. MAYBE SEE YOU LATER.
JESS?
MS. SAWATZKY! HI!
YOU'RE OUT OF HIGH SCHOOL. YOU CAN JUST CALL ME JUDITH NOW.
I WAS JUST THINKING ABOUT YOU, JESS. YOU KNOW, I STILL USE YOUR ESSAY AS AN EXAMPLE WHEN I'M TEACHING MY GRADE TENS. ARE YOU STILL DOING LOTS OF READING?
A BIT... I GUESS MOSTLY STUFF ON THE INTERNET. MY DAD HAS TONS OF BOOKS BUT THEY'RE ALL SO OLD... AND LIKE, ALL BY DEAD WHITE GUYS.
WELL, YOU CAN ALWAYS BORROW FROM ME. I COULD DROP OFF A FEW FAVOURITES AT YOUR HOUSE. WHAT'S YOUR ADDRESS?

OH! THAT WOULD BE AMAZING! WE'RE ON COTTONWOOD DRIVE, NUMBER 1874.

I MIGHT EVEN INCLUDE SOME OLDER ONES. IT'S NOT ALL DEAD WHITE GUYS YOU KNOW.

I WONDER WHAT CANNED FOOD SECTIONS USED TO BE LIKE.

PROBABLY GROSS.

BUT ALSO KIND OF HOPEFUL?

BETTER PACKAGING AT LEAST.

EXCUSE ME.

OH! IS THAT JESS? I DIDN'T RECOGNIZE YOU.

HI MRS NEUFELD.
HOW CAN I HELP YOU?

WELL, I'M LOOKING
FOR CREAM OF
TARTAR.

BUT I ALSO
WANT TO KNOW HOW
YOU'RE DOING.

CREAM OF TARTAR
IS ON AISLE 3.

I'LL TAKE
YOU TO IT.

WE USED TO
SEE YOU IN CHURCH
MORE OFTEN.

BUT YOUR DAD'S THE PASTOR.

SO PERHAPS YOU'RE ALSO ABOVE THE LAWS OF SCRIPTURE.

AH!

THERE YOU GO.

IS THERE SOMETHING ELSE I CAN HELP YOU WITH?

JUST KNOW THAT I'M PRAYING FOR YOU.

YOU'RE CLEARLY NOT PRAYING HARD ENOUGH.

YOU KNOW I RESPECT YOUR FATHER.

BUT GOD'S WORD DOESN'T CHANGE, HOWEVER MUCH WE MIGHT WANT IT TO.

YOU WERE SUCH A SWEET LITTLE GIRL.

I REMEMBER YOU SITTING WITH YOUR OMA EVERY SUNDAY.

WHAT WOULD SHE THINK OF ALL THIS... SPECIAL TREATMENT?

WACK!

HEY, HOW WAS WORK?

FINE.

ACTUALLY...

I HAD AN INTERACTION WITH MRS. NEUFELD.
UH OH.
WITH MY "SINFUL LIFESTYLE" AND YOUR "FALSE TEACHING" WE SEEM TO POSE QUITE A THREAT.

I'M GOING TO GIVE HER A CALL. THIS ISN'T SOMETHING YOU SHOULD HAVE TO DEAL WITH.

I CAN TAKE CARE OF MYSELF, THANKS.

IT WAS WIERD, THOUGH... SHE BROUGHT UP OMA.
WHY WOULD SHE DO THAT?

YOU KNOW, WHAT SHE WOULD THINK OF ALL THE INCLUSION STUFF

LET ME TELL YOU SOMETHING ABOUT YOUR OMA.

YOU KNOW HOW SHE USED TO TEACH IN THAT VILLAGE SOUTH EAST OF TOWN?

WELL, BEFORE SHE DIED, SHE WAS EAGER TO SHARE A MEMORY.

SOMETIMES ON HER WAY HOME FROM WORK SHE WOULD SEE HER MALE COLLEAGUE IN THE TREELINE WITH OPA'S FARMHAND.

SHE'D NEVER TOLD ANYONE ABOUT IT... NOT EVEN YOUR OPA, BUT SHE WANTED ME TO KNOW.
WOAH.

SHE SAID SHE HAD NO PROBLEM WITH THEM AT ALL, SO LONG AS THEY STILL SHOWED UP TO CHURCH EVERY WEEK IN THEIR SUNDAY BEST.
HA HA. NO WAY. I HAVE TO TELL SUSIE.

I SUPPOSE THAT'S ALRIGHT. MAYBE DON'T MENTION THAT HE WORKED FOR OPA.

DON'T MOST OF YOUR FRIENDS LIVE IN THE CITY BY NOW?

YEAH. WELL, NOT SUSIE.

SHE SAID SHE MIGHT BE ABLE TO FIND ME A PROVINCIAL PARKS JOB NEXT SUMMER.

THAT WOULD BE GREAT! YOU ALWAYS LOVED BEING AT CAMP!

IS UH... SUSIE'S FAMILY STILL AT PARK VALLEY?
I THINK SO.

HER FAMILY DOESN'T REALLY TALK TO HER ANYMORE, THOUGH.
REALLY?

HER PARENTS WERE PART OF PARK VALLEY WHEN IT WAS A LOT SMALLER.
BACK WHEN THEY MET AT THE OLD THEATRE ON MAIN STREET.

WHEN YOU WERE YOUNGER WE USED TO GET TOGETHER WITH THEM ONCE IN A WHILE.
YEAH, WE'VE TALKED ABOUT THAT.

I THINK SHE'S A LOT HAPPIER NOW THAT SHE'S ON HER OWN.

LOOKS LIKE THERE'S SOMETHING ON THE PORCH. MORE BAKING FROM KAREN?
I CAN GRAB IT.

JAMES BALDWIN
GIOVANNI'S ROOM
for Jess
URSULA K. LE GUIN
THE DISPOSSESSED

THOUGHT YOU COULD USE A LITTLE BOOST. I KNOW IT'S BEEN A ROUGH FEW WEEKS, WITH HAROLD AND CATHY LEAVING LIKE THAT.

IT'S BEEN ROUGH FOR A LOT OF PEOPLE IN OUR CONGREGATION, ESPECIALLY JESS.
HOW'S SHE DOING?. I MISS HAVING HER IN MY HISTORY CLASS.

OVERALL, I THINK SHE'S ALRIGHT... STILL FIGURING THINGS OUT.

YOU KNOW, THIS IS GOING TO BE MY EIGHTH YEAR TEACHING IN THIS TOWN.

I REMEMBER THINKING I WASN'T MENNONITE ENOUGH TO TAKE THIS JOB.

NOW I'M A TOTAL SNOB ABOUT FARMER SAUSAGE. I EVEN LEARNED HOW TO MAKE MY OWN SCHMAUNT FAT.

HA! WELL, FOR THE RECORD, AS FAR AS I'M CONCERNED, YOU'RE AS MENNONITE AS ANYONE ELSE IS, REGARDLESS OF YOUR CHOLESTEROL.

THERE ARE PEOPLE AROUND HERE WHO TREAT IT LIKE SOME KIND OF BIRTHRIGHT.

IMAGINE TELLING THAT TO THE EARLY ANABAPTISTS!

I LIKED WHAT YOU SAID IN YOUR SERMON LAST SUNDAY...

ABOUT THE CHURCH BEING MADE UP OF PEOPLE WHO'VE BEEN CALLED INTO COMMUNITY.

OF COURSE, FIGURING OUT WHAT THAT MEANS IN OUR OWN TIME AND PLACE IS ALWAYS A CHALLENGE.
RIGHT.

I NEED TO READ MORE THEOLOGY. ANY-THING YOU'D RECOMMEND?

YOU'RE WELCOME TO BORROW SOMETHING FROM MY LIBRARY.

TRY THE SHELF ABOVE ALL THE BIBLE COMMENTARIES.

I CAN VOUCH FOR MOST OF IT. HEHEHE

Stanley Hauerwas
William H. Willimon
Resident Aliens

THIS TITLE ALWAYS INTRIGUED ME.

I DON'T THINK IT'S AGED ALL THAT WELL BUT IT SURE MADE AN IMPACT ON ME WHEN I WAS AT SEMINARY.

I WISH I'D PAID MORE ATTENTION IN BIBLE COLLEGE. TOO MUCH PARTYING HEHEHE.

THERE WAS THIS ONE CLASS I'LL NEVER FORGET CALLED TRUTH AND LIES - IT WAS MORE OF A PHILOSOPHY COURSE.

BUT BECAUSE OF THE TITLE IT ATTRACTED A LOT OF THE MORE... UH... CONSERVATIVE STUDENTS.

MOST OF THEM WANTED TO TALK ABOUT THE BIBLE —WHETHER IT WAS INERRANT AND SO ON.

BUT IN THE LAST CLASS OF THE SEM-ESTER, THIS GUY—I THINK HIS NAME WAS DAVID—USED HIS PRESENTATION TO COME OUT.

HOW DID YOUR CLASS REACT?
IT WAS MIXED BUT SEVERAL OF US CLAPPED... INCLUDING THE PROFESSOR.

I REMEMBER SOMEONE SAYING SOME-THING LIKE "THANK YOU FOR SHARING YOUR TRUTH."

BUT AT THE TIME I THOUGHT THAT MISSED SOMETHING IMPORTANT.

IT WAS ALSO OUR TRUTH.

IN THAT MOMENT WE WERE THE ONES BEING JUDGED.

ANYWAY. I SHOULD BE GOING.

THANKS FOR THE BOOK.

KNOCK
KNOCK

I GOT IT, DAD.

HI SUSIE.
HI MR. SUDERMAN.

WE'RE GOING OUT FOR FRIES AND ICE CREAM.
WANT US TO GRAB YOU SOMETHING?

I'M GOOD, THANKS.

CLICK

KSH! KSH!

SH
KSH

VRR VRR
CLICK
KSHHH
UPCOMING EVENTS

KAREN, COULD YOU RUN THESE BULLETINS TO THE GREETER-USHERS?
SORRY I DIDN'T HAVE THEM OUT SOONER.

GERHARD, DON'T YOU, UM, THINK THIS IS A BIT... EXTREME?
WE'RE GOING TO ALIENATE PEOPLE REGARDLESS.
WELCOME TO JUBILEE MENNONITE CHURCH
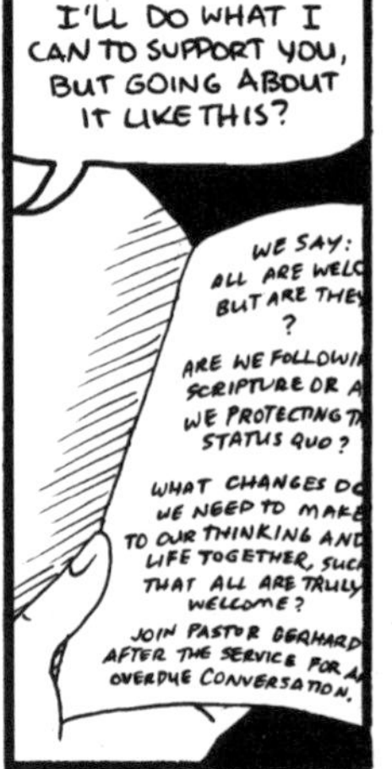
I'LL DO WHAT I CAN TO SUPPORT YOU, BUT GOING ABOUT IT LIKE THIS?
WE SAY:
ALL ARE WELC
BUT ARE THEY
?
ARE WE FOLLOWI
SCRIPTURE OR A
WE PROTECTING T
STATUS QUO?
WHAT CHANGES DO
WE NEED TO MAKE
TO OUR THINKING AND
LIFE TOGETHER, SUCH
THAT ALL ARE TRULY
WELCOME?
JOIN PASTOR GERHARD
AFTER THE SERVICE FOR A
OVERDUE CONVERSATION.

I JUST WANT TO HAVE A CONVERSATION.

KING OF
PRINCE OF

REMEMBRANCE DAY

YOU
CAN

OKAY LET'S REVIEW.
N17

WHICH CONCEPT DO THE GREAT WARS OF THE 20TH CENTURY PUT INTO QUESTION?
UHH... TRUTH?
zeitgeist
ideology

PROGRESS
TAP
TAP

PROGRESS.

THE IDEA THAT HUMAN ACHIEVEMENT IN THINGS LIKE TECHNOLOGY WILL BRING WITH IT INCREASED PROSPERITY AND PEACE.
SNAP

AN END TO SCARCITY AND, WITH IT, AN END TO CONFLICT; THAT HISTORY MOVES FORWARD IN A STRAIGHT LINE.

I WANT YOU ALL TO THINK ABOUT THAT THIS WEEK AS WE APPROACH REMEMBRANCE DAY.

WHO ENDS UP FIGHTING IN THESE WARS?
AND WHO ULTIMATELY GETS TO BENEFIT FROM THEM?
zeitgeist
ideology
ENLIGHTENMENT
ATTENDENCE

YOU CAN MAKE IT
N17

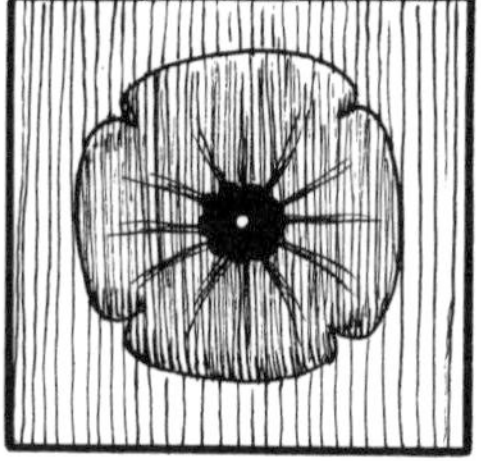

PETE!
HEY JUDITH!

CLASSES GOING WELL?
OH, NOT BAD.

WE'RE READING THE OUTSIDERS RIGHT NOW.
OH, I LOVE CAMUS!
NO. OUTSIDERS WITH AN "S." BY S.E. HINTON.
BUT THIS TIME OF YEAR IS ALWAYS A BIT HARD AND AWKWARD.
THIS TIME OF YEAR?
YOU KNOW.
THE MENNONITE THING.
RIGHT. SOMETIMES I FORGET WHERE I'M TEACHING.
IT'S FINE.
I GREW UP HEARING THE STORIES OF CONSCIENTIOUS OBJECTORS FROM MY GRANDPA. I USED TO BE PRETTY ZEALOUS ABOUT IT.

THAT SOUNDS SO INSPIRING! WITH A GRANDPA LIKE THAT I WOULD HAVE BEEN ZEALOUS TOO.
I DON'T DOUBT IT.

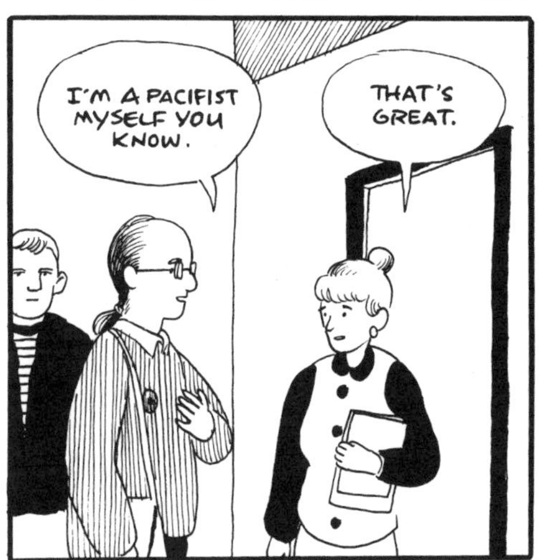
I'M A PACIFIST MYSELF YOU KNOW.
THAT'S GREAT.

WE'LL HAVE TO TALK ABOUT IT MORE SOME TIME.

NOW WHERE WAS I GOING AGAIN?

RIGHT. THE PARKING LOT.

RICK! DEBRA!

WHAT'S GOING ON?!

SORRY, CORPORAL STEVENS.
PLEASE GIVE US A MOMENT.
MA'AM

CAN WE HELP YOU, PETE?

WELL, TO START WITH, YOU CAN TELL ME WHAT THESE MACHINES OF WAR ARE DOING ON THE FRONT LAWN OF OUR HIGH SCHOOL!

AND WHY IT LOOKS LIKE THERE'S A RECRUITMENT BOOTH BEING SET UP!

PETE, CALM YOURSELF. THIS IS JUST PART OF OUR REMEMBRANCE DAY CEREMONY THIS YEAR.

AS YOU KNOW, RICK, OUR NEW ENGLISH TEACHER HAS SERVED IN THE MILITARY.
DULCE ET DECORUM EST.

HE SET THE WHOLE THING UP FOR US.

IT WAS THE LEAST I COULD DO, ESPECIALLY CONSIDERING OUR COUNTRY IS AT WAR.

OUR TROOPS NEED OUR SUPPORT NOW MORE THAN EVER.

IT'S ABOUT TIME THIS COMMUNITY STARTED PULLING ITS WEIGHT.
AND YES, I'VE READ WILFRED OWEN.

BUT DEBRA, YOU'RE MENNONITE.

PACIFISM IS, LIKE, THE ONLY THING YOU ALL AGREE ON.

AND, YOU KNOW, DISTRUSTING THE GOVERNMENT.

I'M NOT GOING TO DEBATE THIS WITH YOU, PETE.

AHEM.

WE'RE A PUBLIC SCHOOL.

WE'RE PART OF A COUNTRY WITH A MILITARY.

YES. THIS TOWN HAS A HISTORY OF CONSCIENTIOUS OBJECTION.

BUT PEOPLE HERE FOUGHT IN BOTH WARS.

AND THOSE WHO MANAGED TO SURVIVE – OUR VETERANS – RETURNED TO A COMMUNITY THAT ALL BUT REJECTED THEM.
SIGN UP
TODAY

THANKS FOR THE HISTORY LESSON, DEBRA.

LAST I CHECKED, THE WHOLE POINT OF HAVING REMEMBRANCE DAY WAS TO COUNTER THE GLOR-IFICATION OF WAR.

YOU KNOW THAT IS NOT WHAT WE'RE DOING. THIS CONVERSATION IS OVER.

SORRY ABOUT THAT, RICK.
IT'S FINE. YOU CAN'T REASON WITH PEOPLE LIKE THAT.

SLAM!!!!
FORD

ASSHOLES!

24

← Judith

8:45PM

Hey, we should have that chat soon
6:30PM

Ya! That'd be great!
8:27PM

Did you see the front lawn at school today?
8:27PM

OMG yes!! :(
8:29PM

I'm furious. It's so irresponsible!!!
8:30PM

SEND

CLICK

CLICK

NO TALENT SHOW TODAY MR. DAVIS.
HA! GOOD ONE.

HIGH
COMES YOU!

PETE?
HEY JUDITH.

YOU BROUGHT YOUR GUITAR.
DO YOU PLAY?

I USED TO.

EXACTLY.

YOU'RE WELCOME TO JOIN ME.

I'M OFF TO FIGHT THE MILITARY INDUSTRIAL COMPLEX THE OLD FASHIONED WAY.

GOTTA GET OUT THERE BEFORE THE STUDENTS START ARRIVING.

PETE, DO YOU ACTUALLY THINK THIS IS A GOOD IDEA?

I WROTE MY FAIR SHARE OF PROTEST SONGS DURING THE BUSH YEARS.

JOIN TODAY!
BE PART OF THE SOLUTION
MAKE A REAL DIFFERENCE
CANADIAN FORCES

WE'LL TELL THEM WE LOVE THEM WITH BOMBS...

EXPLOSIONS AND BULLET SHELLS...

WILL BLOW THEM ALL TO HELL...

WE'LL SPREAD THE LOVE OF JESUS...

...WITH BOMBS...

'CAUSE CHRISTIANITY ONLY LIVES IN DEMOCRACY, AND DEMOCRACY'S CREATED WITH BOMBS.
LOL. MR. DAVIS, OUR HERO.
WOOOO
THIS IS AMAZING.

AS THE DEER

SNIFF
SNIFF

CLINK
CLINK

I CAN'T BELIEVE MIKE IS A PASTOR AT THAT NEW MEGA CHURCH.
HAHA I KNOW.
Tommy Douglas

HE WAS, LIKE, THE FIRST PERSON IN OUR GRADE TO GET DRUNK.

DO YOU REMEMBER WHEN HE MOONED OUR VOLLEYBALL TEAM?
Tommy Douglas

AND RACHEL MOONED HIM RIGHT BACK, AND SHE WAS SUSPENDED.
HAHA

I SHOULD PROBABLY HEAD BACK TO TOWN. IT LOOKS LIKE IT'S GETTING WORSE.

WE SHOULD GET TOGETHER AGAIN DURING THE HOLIDAYS. I'LL NEED A BREAK FROM ALL THE FAMILY GATHERINGS.
I HAVEN'T BEEN TO ONE OF THOSE IN AGES. AFTER MY GRANDPARENTS DIED, NO ONE REALLY KEPT IT UP.
BUT I'LL DEFINITELY NEED A BREAK TOO. I KNOW MY FOLKS ARE EXPECTING ME TO JOIN THEM FOR ALL THE CHRISTMAS STUFF AT THEIR CHURCH.
YOUR FAMILY IS MORE CONSERVATIVE, RIGHT?
IT'S... A MIXED BAG.
MY PARENTS' SIDES OF THE FAMILY ARE PRETTY DIFFERENT, EVEN THOUGH THEY'RE BOTH MENNO.
OH?

I'VE BEEN DOING SOME RESEARCH LATELY — MY GRAND-PARENTS COULDN'T SPEAK MUCH ENGLISH, SO I HAD TO PIECE TO-GETHER A LOT OF STUFF ON MY OWN.

DIFFERENT MIGRATIONS, EAST RESERVE, WEST RESERVE ...YOU KNOW HOW IT IS.
UH... NOT REALLY.

OH, SORRY.

IT'S PRETTY INTENSE... HAHA.

...ANYWAY...

TO ANSWER YOUR QUESTION YEAH, MY PARENTS' CHURCH SPLIT OFF THE MAIN CONFERENCE A LONG TIME AGO BECAUSE IT WAS BECOMING TOO WORLDLY.

BUT MOST OF MY FAMILY ARE AT PARK VALLEY NOW ...HANGING OUT WITH PASTOR MIKE.
IF THEY ONLY KNEW, HAHA.

THANKS FOR THE VISIT.
DRIVE SAFE.

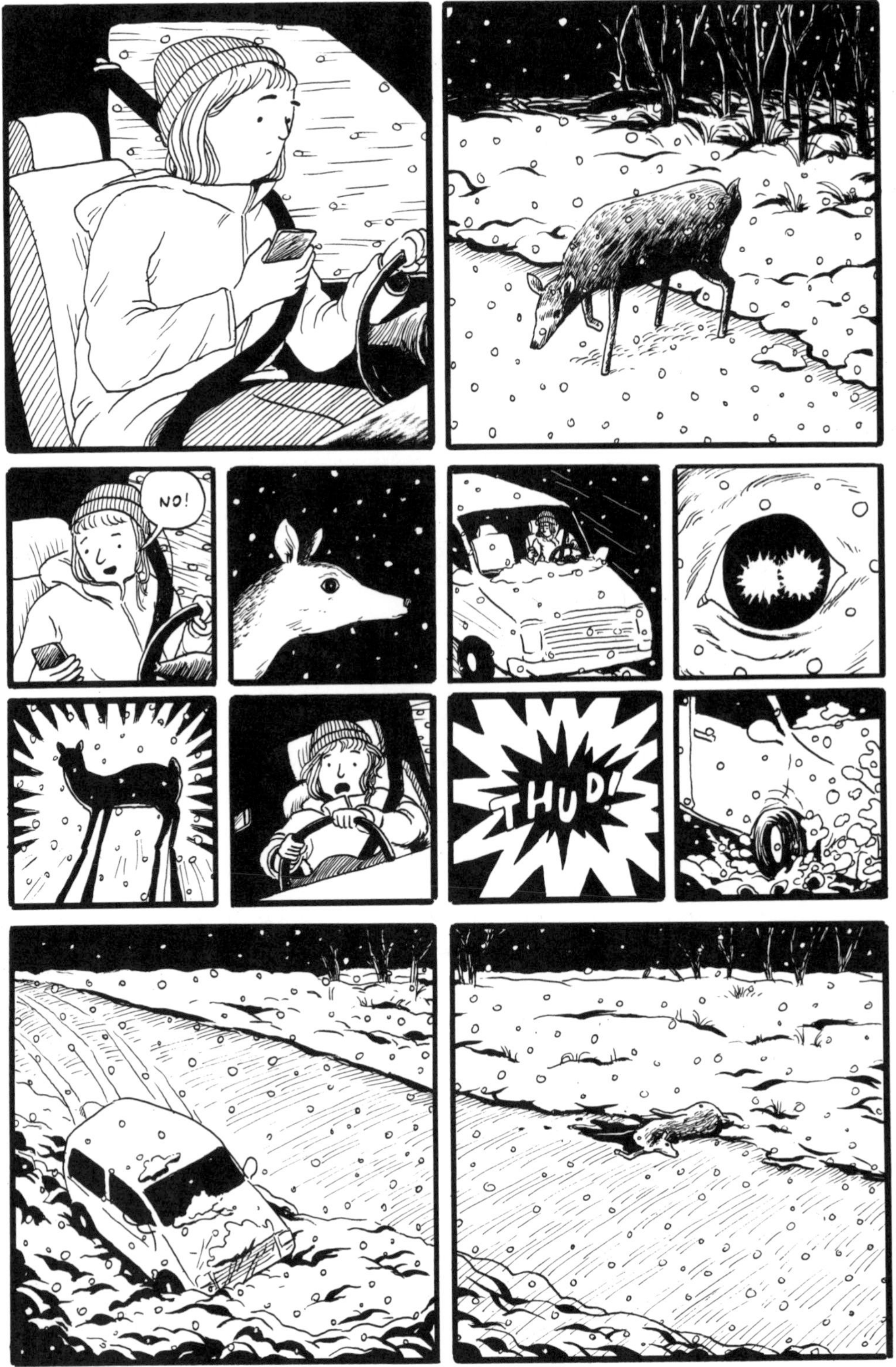
NO!
THUD!

Powering off...

SHIT.
SHIT.
SHIT.
VRRRRRR
RRRRRRR
SHIT.
I HAVE TO LEAVE. I'M SORRY.

KNOCK
KNOCK

CAN I HELP YOU?
HI THERE.

I HIT A DEER. ON THE HIGHWAY AND NOW MY CAR IS STUCK. CAN I USE YOUR PHONE?
OH MY! YES OF COURSE. COME RIGHT IN.

MY WIFE IS MAKING A POT OF TEA. WOULD YOU LIKE SOME?
SURE THAT'D BE GREAT.

I'M HAROLD.
JUDITH. NICE TO MEET YOU. THANKS SO MUCH FOR DOING THIS.
OH, IT'S NO PROBLEM AT ALL.

PLEASE, TAKE A SEAT. I'LL GO GET THE PHONE.

HERE YOU GO.
THANKS, AGAIN.

I CALLED CAA BUT THEY WON'T COME UNTIL TOMORROW.

I CAN DRIVE YOU TO THE ACCIDENT SITE TOMORROW.
THIS IS SO KIND OF YOU.
YOU CAN SPEND THE NIGHT HERE.
SO WHAT DO YOU DO FOR A LIVING, JUDITH?
OH, I TEACH AT THE HIGH SCHOOL IN TOWN.
OH REALLY? WHAT'S YOUR LAST NAME?
UM, SAWATZKY.
YOUR FATHER'S NAME IS GEORGE?
AND YOUR MOTHER IS ANITA?
YES.
I WAS IN THE SAME CLASS AS YOUR UNCLE PETER DURING HIGH SCHOOL.
SORRY, I'M STILL A BIT SHAKEN UP FROM THE ACCIDENT. I CAN'T STOP THINKING ABOUT THAT DEER.

IT'S HARD TO SEE THOSE DEER AT THE BEST OF TIMES, LET ALONE IN A SNOWSTORM.

WE CAN THANK GOD IT WASN'T ANOTHER VEHICLE.

JUDITH, IS YOUR FAMILY STILL PART OF THE BMF CHURCH IN TOWN?
YEAH, BUT LATELY MOST OF THEM HAVE BEEN ATTENDING PARK VALLEY.

YOU KNOW THE BIG CHURCH ON THE SOUTH EDGE OF TOWN? I GUESS IT'S PRETTY NEW.

OH, YES! WE'RE ACTUALLY LOOKING FOR A NEW CHURCH RIGHT NOW. WE SHOULD GIVE IT A TRY.

MAYBE WE'D SEE YOU THERE!
MAYBE.

WE WERE PART OF JUBILEE MENNONITE FOR A LONG TIME, AND WE'LL MISS THEIR CONNECTION TO THE PEACE TRADITION, BUT ON OTHER ISSUES THEY'VE BECOME FAR TOO WORLDLY.

I APPRECIATE THAT BMF STILL HOLDS TO A PEACE POSITION. THE SAME CAN'T BE SAID FOR SOME OF THE OTHER DENOMENATIONS.

I'VE ALWAYS APPRECIATED THAT TOO.

I DON'T KNOW IF YOU HEARD ABOUT WHAT HAPPENED AT THE HIGH SCHOOL ON REMEMBRANCE DAY.

SOME OF THE STAFF HAD ARRANGED FOR REAL ARTILLERY TO BE BROUGHT TO THE SCHOOL AND DISPLAYED.

THEY'D EVEN SET UP A BOOTH FOR RECRUITMENT!

OH DEAR.
THAT WOULD HAVE BEEN UNTHINKABLE A FEW DECADES AGO.

BUT YOU KNOW, THERE WERE MENNO-NITES HERE WHO WENT TO WAR.
YES, I WISH I KNEW MORE OF THAT HISTORY.

I'M SURE YOU'VE HEARD HOW PAINFUL AND DIVI-SIVE IT WAS.

MY UNCLE JOINED UP AS A PLANE MECHANIC.

YOU COULD ARGUE THAT HE WAS NO MORE USEFUL TO THE WAR EFFORT THAN THOSE WHO DID ALTERNATIVE SERVICE.

BUT EVEN THOUGH HE TECHNICALLY DIDN'T FIGHT HE WAS EXCOMMUNICATED.

THERE WAS ALSO A LOT OF ANTI-GERMAN SENTIMENT DIRECTED AT MENNONITES IN THOSE DAYS. PEOPLE QUESTIONING THEIR ALLEGIANCES.

AND MANY OF US WERE BORN AND RAISED RIGHT HERE. MY PARENTS REFRAINED FROM SPEAKING ANY LOW GERMAN IN THE HOUSE OUT OF LOYALTY TO CANADA.

MY OLDER BROTHER APPLIED TO BE A CONSCIENTIOUS OBJECTOR BUT THE JUDGE HAD A CHIP ON HIS SHOULDER AND WANTED TO MAKE AN EXAMPLE OF HIM. SO MY BROTHER'S APPLICATION WAS REJECTED.

WHEN HE WOULDN'T COMPLY, THEY SENT HIM TO PRISON WHERE THEY TRIED TO CONVINCE HIM HE'D ALREADY SIGNED ON. THEY STARVED HIM, BEAT HIM AND TOLD HIM HE WAS A NAZI.

BUT HE WOULDN'T GO. AFTER TWO YEARS, HE RECEIVED A DISHONOURABLE DIS-CHARGE AND RETURNED HOME. HE WAS SO WORN DOWN I BARELY RECOGNIZED HIM.

BECAUSE HE NEVER GOT C.O. STATUS, HE WAS NEVER RECOGNIZED BY HIS CHURCH OR THE WIDER COMMUNITY.

FOR YEARS, I WAS BITTER, BUT I REALIZED EVENTUALLY THAT HIS MIS-TREATMENT DIDN'T DIMINISH THE EFFORTS OF OTHER C.O.S.

I WAS JUST A BOY AT THE TIME, BUT I STILL REMEMBER THOSE MEN COMING BACK FROM ALTERNATIVE SERVICE.

HOW RELIEVED WE ALL WERE TO SEE THEM AGAIN.

SO MANY FROM THE NEXT TOWN OVER – MOSTLY ENGLISH AND FRENCH – NEVER MADE IT BACK.

I KNOW SOME OF THEM FELT FUTILE, OR EVEN GUILTY, FOR NOT GOING OVERSEAS TO FIGHT; BUT IN THAT MOMENT, I KNEW IT WAS WORTH IT.
THEY COULD REST ASSURED THAT THEY'D FOLLOWED GOD'S COMMANDMENT.
WE NEED TO REMEMBER THERE ARE ALTERNATIVES TO WAR.
JUDITH, DO YOU HAVE ANY C.O.s IN YOUR FAMILY?
I DID.
MY OPA WAS A FARMER, WHICH MADE HIM EXEMPT FROM THE MILITARY.
MY OTHER GRANDPA WAS A C.O. IT'S HOW HE GOT HIS START AS A TEACHER.
SO TEACHING RUNS IN THE FAMILY!

JUDITH, WHAT'S WRONG?

RECENTLY I LEARNED THAT HIS POSTING WAS AT AN INDIAN RESIDENTIAL SCHOOL.
HE NEVER TALKED ABOUT IT WHEN HE WAS ALIVE.

I'M SURE HIS INTENTIONS WERE GOOD...
IT'S STILL BETTER THAN GOING TO WAR.

IS IT? WE SURE CAN'T CALL IT PEACE.

NOT WHEN WE KNOW WHAT HAPPENED AT THOSE SCHOOLS, WHY THEY EXISTED IN THE FIRST PLACE.

IT WAS ONLY A DROP IN THE BUCKET – OTHER DENOMENATIONS WERE FAR WORSE.

IN MY GRANDPA'S CASE, IT WAS A SCHOOL RUN BY THE UNITED CHURCH.

MENNONITES FILLED SPOTS LEFT BY MEN WHO WENT TO FIGHT, AND WE TAUGHT AT OTHER SCHOOLS TOO.

I'M SORRY. YOU'RE BEING SO GENEROUS WITH ME – I SHOULDN'T BE BURDENING YOU WITH THIS!

I KNOW IT'S NOT SOMETHING WE LIKE TO TALK ABOUT. MY FAMILY'S MADE THAT PRETTY CLEAR.
NO. YOU'RE RIGHT TO MENTION IT. WE'RE SO ACCUSTOMED TO SEEING OURSELVES AS EXCEPTIONS.
WE SHOULD BE GETTING TO BED.
JUDITH, YOU MUST BE A FINE TEACHER.
I'LL TAKE YOU TO THE GUEST ROOM.

BLOOM WHERE YOU'RE PLANTED

HESPELER: A TOWN, A
MANITOBA MENNONITE CENTENNIA
SAINTS and SINNERS
MARTYRS MIRROR
Thieleman J.
WIEBE · PEACE SHALL DESTR
Building on the Past

OH SHIT. I WAS GONNA MEET WITH PETE TOMORROW MORNING.
FLIP FLIP

St. Agathe, 88
Saskatchewan, 17
Sawatzky, John, 192
Sawatzky, Klaas, 193
Schanzenfeld 3, 41, 85
Schism, church 20, 56

espeler conscientious objectors

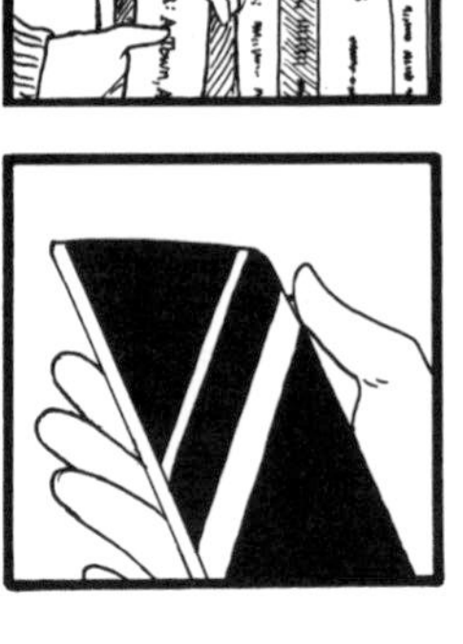

UGH.
I'M THE WORST.

YAWN

Judith
Perfect. I'll be there at 10am.
3:30pm
Hey, looking forward to coffee today. See you soon!
Send

TAP TAP

HMM...
WHAT'S THE DEAL, JUDITH?

AH, THERE IT IS.
IT'S WORSE THAN I REALIZED.

HUFF HUFF

HUFF

HEY!

GO EASY ON YOURSELF, HAROLD.
THOUGHT MAYBE WE COULD GET IT OUT ON OUR OWN.

THE GUY FROM CAA SAID HE SHOULD BE HERE IN A FEW MINUTES.

IT'S GONNA TAKE A WHILE BUT THEY'LL BRING IT RIGHT TO THE AUTOSHOP.
WHERE SHOULD I DROP YOU IN THE MEANTIME?

THE COFFEE SHOP IS FINE. MAYBE HE'S STILL THERE.
I COULD ALSO USE A WARM DRINK.

SO MANY TRUCKS. I WONDER WHAT IT'S ALL FOR.
LOOKS LIKE OIL PIPELINES.

JUDITH! OVER HERE!

SORRY PETE!
NO PROBLEM. I WAS JUST A LITTLE WORRIED.

I HAD AN UNFORTUNATE RUN-IN WITH A DEER LAST NIGHT. MY CAR FARED BETTER THAN THE DEER, BUT I HIT THE DITCH.
AND THEN MY PHONE DIED.

THIS IS HAROLD - HE AND HIS WIFE TOOK ME IN AFTER THE ACCIDENT.

HAROLD! GOOD TO SEE YOU!

PASTOR GERHARD, I HOPE THERE ARE NO HARD FEELINGS.
OF COURSE NOT.
IF IT WAS UP TO ME, WE...
YOU HAVE CONVICTIONS, JUST LIKE I DO.

I KNOW YOU'RE TRYING TO SHEPHERD YOUR FLOCK THE BEST WAY YOU KNOW HOW.
PERHAPS WE JUST AREN'T READY TO BE CHALLENGED ON CERTAIN ISSUES.

IF THAT CHANGES YOU LET ME KNOW.

NICE TO SEE YOU ALL.

TWO LATTES TO GO, AND A CHAI LATTE TO STAY.

YOU TAKE CARE, JUDITH. I HOPE WE'LL SEE YOU AGAIN.

THANKS AGAIN... FOR EVERYTHING.

ALL OF OUR FAMILY STORIES HAVE PARTS WE WISH WERE DIFFERENT.

BUT THAT'S NO REASON TO RUN AWAY FROM YOUR HERITAGE.
WE'RE A HUMBLE PEOPLE BUT WE HAVE A LOT TO BE PROUD OF, YOU INCLUDED.
YOU KNOW HAROLD?
HE AND HIS WIFE CATHY USED TO ATTEND MY CHURCH.
GERHARD, THE PASTOR, REALLY STUCK HIS NECK OUT TO MAKE IT MORE INCLUSIVE.
THE NEUFELDS WEREN'T THE ONLY ONES WHO LEFT.

BUT AT LEAST WE'RE FINALLY ON THE RIGHT TRACK.
JUDITH?
SORRY... I'M LISTENING.
I WISH IT WAS THAT SIMPLE.

PAPER BIRD

HI, CAN WE, UM HELP YOU?

JUST DOING A BIT OF FORAGING. THERE USED TO BE LOTS OF MUSHROOMS AROUND HERE.

SORRY—I'M REBECCA. MY FAMILY USED TO LIVE ON THIS PROPERTY... IT'S BEEN A WHILE SINCE I'VE VISITED.
YOU SURE YOU KNOW WHICH ONES ARE SAFE TO EAT?
OH! YOU MUST BE THE PETERS GIRL. WELL YOU'RE ALWAYS WELCOME HERE.

YEAH, I'M PRETTY CAREFUL. I'VE ACTUALLY TAKEN A COURSE ON MYCOLOGY.
YOU KNOW THERE MIGHT BE MORE MUSH-ROOMS FURTHER DOWN THE TREELINE.

GOOD LUCK!

HEY!

I WAS WORRIED YOU WOULDN'T MAKE IT.

HOW WAS YOUR TIME WITH YOUR MOM?
OH, FINE.

I WENT TO LOOK FOR MUSHROOMS AT ONE OF MY OLD SPOTS,
NEAR THE FAMILY FARM.

CLAP
CLAP

THEY'RE TEARING UP STREETS AGAIN, THEY'RE BUILDING A NEW HOTEL
WOOO!
CLAP
WOOO!
CLAP
WOOOO!

THE MAYOR'S OUT KILLING KIDS TO KEEP TAXES DOWN

AND ME AND MY ANGER SIT FOLDING A PAPER BIRD

LETTING THE CURTAINS TURN TO BEATING WINGS

WHAT'S UP? YOU OK?

THEY'RE INSTALLING NEW PIPELINES WHERE I GREW UP, WHERE MY DAD GREW UP.
REALLY?!

I SAW THEM SITTING THERE WHEN I WAS OUT NEAR THE FARM.

THEY'RE RIPPING EVERYTHING UP. AND THE PEOPLE OUT THERE ARE JUST LETTING IT HAPPEN.

I NEED TO SEE IT.

YOU WILL

I'LL TAKE YOU THIS WEEKEND.

I THINK I'M GOING TO HEAD HOME EARLY.
YOU SHOULD STAY, THOUGH.
YOU SURE?

I KNOW YOU WANT TO SING ALONG TO "ONE GREAT CITY."
I'LL SING FOR BOTH OF US.

SNAP

HEY, THERE HE IS.

BEERS AT THE RIVER?

COME ON, JASON. WE NEVER SEE YOU ANY-MORE.
I GUESS IT'S NOT THAT LATE.

BEER
VENDOR

BEER
VENDOR

THAT WAS CLOSE. YOU OKAY?
SMACK!
YA, I'M FINE.

NICE ONE, ANDY.
ALWAYS WANTED TO DO THAT.

PFFF
PFFF

REMEMBER WHEN WE USED TO HAVE FIRES OUT HERE?

ME AND EVAN ARE GOING TO AN-OTHER SHOW NEXT WEEKEND. YOU SHOULD COME.
YEAH, BRING REBECCA. IT WAS GOOD TO SEE HER.

WE ALREADY MADE PLANS... DRIVING OUT TO SEE HER MOM.
OUT WHERE?

HESPELER

MAN, I DIDN'T KNOW REBECCA WAS FROM THERE. SHE'S SO, LIKE... NORMAL.

SORRY, HAHA... YOU KNOW WHAT I MEAN... SHE'S INTO COOL SHIT!
OH YEAH?

THE ONES WHO ESCAPE ARE ALWAYS KIND OF BADASS, I GUESS.
SHE STILL HAS FRIENDS THERE.

ANDY, I THINK YOU'RE IMAGINING, LIKE, REALLY TRADITIONAL MENNONITES. OLD ORDER... IS THAT WHAT THEY'RE CALLED?

I'VE ALWAYS BEEN CURIOUS ABOUT THAT STUFF.
MY MOM'S FAMILY IS MENNONITE. BUT EVEN JUST ON HER SIDE THERE ARE A FEW DIFFERENT KINDS.
BUZZ
BUZZ

AND THEY ALL THINK THEY'RE THE "RIGHT" ONES.

Still at the show?
10:06
Thought you were coming over.
10:47
This is the last night before my roommate gets back.
11:33
Type message

SORRY, I GOTTA GO.
AW, COME ON, MAN...

HEY JASON, I WANTED TO ASK YOU - CAN YOU TAKE A LOOK AT MY BIKE THIS WEEK? THE BRAKES ARE ALL MESSED UP.
UGH.

BRING IT TO THE SHOP. I'LL BE THERE.
THINK YOU COULD GET ME A DEAL?

SEEYA GUYS.

CRUNCH

THANKS FOR SIGNALLING, ASSHOLE!

HEY!

YOU'RE LISTENING TO CBC RADIO 1— THAT'S 89.3 FM IN WINNIPEG WHERE WE'RE BRINGING YOU UP TO SPEED.
UP NEXT: A MAYOR IN SOUTHERN MANITOBA IS WELCOMING A BOOST TO THE LOCAL ECONOMY.

A PIPELINE PROJECT BRINGS HUNDREDS OF JOBS AND WORKERS TO OUR TOWN—

AND BENEFITS OUR ENTIRE COMMUNITY.

EACH WORKER NEEDS A PLACE TO STAY. THEY MAY NEED BREAKFAST OR DINNER, THEY'LL BE SHOPPING FOR SERVICES LOCALLY DURING THEIR OFF HOURS.

BUZZ BUZZ

UP NEXT WE'VE GOT

YA, I'LL BE DRIVING OUT TONIGHT WITH JASON — WAS THERE ANY THING YOU WANTED US TO GRAB ON THE WAY?

YES, WE CAN STAY IN SEPARATE ROOMS, IF THAT MAKES YOU FEEL BETTER.
THAT'S JASON AT THE DOOR... GOTTA GO.

HEY BABE -SMELLS AMAZING IN HERE.

WHAT TIME DID YOU WANT TO GET GOING?
I WANT TO GET THERE BY NINE, SO WE SHOULD LEAVE PRETTY SOON.

MY MOM IS THRILLED THAT YOU'RE FINALLY STAYING OVER. SHE'S ALWAYS LOOKING FOR AN EXCUSE TO MAKE WAFFLES.

I LIKE KAREN. SHE'S—
EMBARRASSING?

I WAS GONNA SAY "ENTHUSIASTIC!"

WE CAN'T STAY TOO LONG. THERE'S STUFF WE STILL NEED TO DO IN THE CITY THIS WEEKEND.
LIKE WHAT?
PENNER
PENNER

WELL, I GOT A FLAT YESTERDAY.
ANOTHER ONE?!
THERE'S ALSO THIS CLICKING SOUND WHEN I PEDAL.

AND I'M NOT DONE MY TERM PAPER. I NEED YOU TOO LOOK AT IT WHEN WE GET BACK. IT'S DUE ON MONDAY.

SORRY... I KNOW EVERYBODY'S ALWAYS ASKING YOU TO DO THINGS FOR THEM, ESPECIALLY ME.

YEAH, HAH. I MEAN, I DON'T MIND SO MUCH WHEN ITS FOR YOU.

AND IT'S FINE WITH ME IF WE HEAD BACK EARLIER. BEING OUT HERE IS A BIT WEIRD FOR ME.

I'M EXCITED FOR YOU TO SEE THE FARM.

YOU KNOW THE FOLKS WHO RUN IT NOW, RIGHT?
NOT REALLY, BUT LAST WEEK I RAN INTO THEM AND WE CHATTED.

IT'LL BE FINE. THEY SAID I'M ALWAYS WELCOME THERE.

MY FAMILY USED TO TAKE ME ON DAY TRIPS OUT HERE WHEN I WAS A KID.

WE'D VISIT THIS SITE WHERE MY RELATIVES USED TO LIVE.
WE SHOULD TRY TO LOOK FOR IT!

MAYBE. IF YOU WANNA GET BACK WE PROBABLY DON'T HAVE TIME.

AND BESIDES, I'M SORT OF AFRAID TO SEE WHAT'S BECOME OF IT.

THERE'S ALL THIS OTHER STUFF TO CONTEND WITH, YOU KNOW?

CROP OF
ROUND UP
BE GRATEFUL

HERE WE GO.

HEY MOM.

HI KAREN

I'M GLAD YOU'RE STAYING FOR THE WEEKEND - WE'VE GOT LOTS TO DO!

YA, TOTALLY. WE HAVE SOME THINGS WE WANT TO DO TOO,

I'D LIKE TO SHOW JASON THE FARM.

MY FAMILY ACTUALLY LIVED AROUND THESE PARTS FOR A WHILE.

I THOUGHT BECAUSE YOU'RE...

...

MÉTIS?

YES, SORRY, I THOUGHT THAT MEANT YOU WERE FROM ANOTHER PART OF THE PROVINCE.

MY FATHER WOULD ALWAYS TELL US WE WERE FARMING THE LAND THAT NO ONE ELSE WANTED.

WE'VE TALKED ABOUT THIS, MOM.

THE LAND WASN'T EMPTY BEFORE OUR ANCESTORS GOT HERE.

JASON SAID THERE WAS A TRADING POST JUST A MILE OUT OF TOWN.

THAT'S WHAT BROUGHT MY GREAT GRAND-PARENTS' FAMILIES THIS WAY.

MY RELATIVES WERE FORCED OUT WHEN MENNONITES STARTED SETTLING HERE.
BUT SOME STAYED.

IT'S CLEAR CANADA HAD ITS OWN AGENDA FOR THIS AREA.

I DIDN'T EVEN TAKE YOUR COATS!
WE'RE BOTH PRETTY TIRED.

THERE ARE TOWELS AND FRESH SHEETS ON YOUR BEDS.

THANKS KAREN.

UGH... SORRY ABOUT THAT. MY MOM—SHE MEANS WELL.

SHE'S STILL GETTING USED TO THIS STUFF.
I KNOW, BUT NONE OF THIS "STUFF" IS NEW INFORMATION.

I WISH PEOPLE WOULD JUST DO SOME OF THIS SHIT THEMSELVES.

THEIR MINDS ALWAYS GO BLANK AS SOON AS YOU GO BACK A GENERATION OR TWO.

I SHOULD GET TO MY ROOM. MY MOM'S PROB-ABLY WAITING TO HEAR MY DOOR CLOSE.

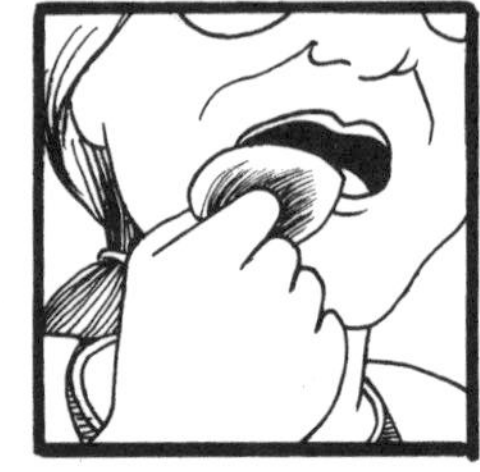

CRUNCH
CRUNCH
A HISTORY OF THE MANITOBA ACT

GOOD MORNING!
HOW'D YOU SLEEP?

UH... FINE, THANKS.
SCRATCH

THERE'S COFFEE AND CEREAL, OR I COULD MAKE YOU SOME WAFFLES.

MOM, I THINK WE'RE GONNA HEAD OUT RIGHT AWAY.

OH. I SEE.

BYE!
IT WOULD BE NICE IF WE COULD ALL HAVE DINNER.

WE SHOULD BE BACK IN TIME.
WE'LL GRAB A BOTTLE OF WINE.

DON'T WORRY ABOUT ME—I HAVE PLENTY TO DO IN THE GARDEN.

BYE, MOM!

YOU'RE SURE THIS IS OKAY?
JASON — IF IT WAS GOING TO BE WEIRD I WOULDN'T TAKE YOU.
WE LIVED HERE UNTIL I WAS FOURTEEN.

I JUST FEEL A BIT UNCOMFORTABLE. THESE PEOPLE DON'T KNOW ME.
AND IT'S NOT LIKE THEY'RE EXPECTING US.
IT'LL BE FINE. TRUST ME, OK?
BARK BARK

HEY BUDDY.

JASON! OVER HERE!

THIS WAS MY FAVOURITE PLACE TO HIDE.
I STASHED TREASURES IN THE WALLS.

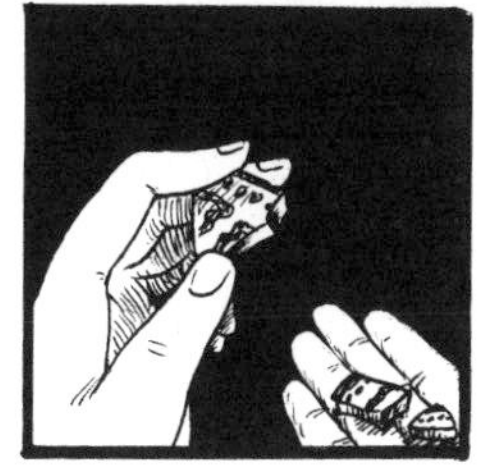

I COLLECTED THESE FROM THE FIELD BEHIND THE BARN.

MAYBE WE SHOULD RETURN THEM.
I LIKE THAT IDEA

OH GOD, I FORGOT...

HOW DO YOU FORGET SOMETHING LIKE THIS?

IT'S SO WEIRD SEEING THIS HAPPENING ON A FARM.

LIKE, ISN'T THIS THE LAST PLACE YOU'D WANT OIL TO BE FLOWING?

YOU'D THINK SO, BUT...

THIS IS A REPLACEMENT, REMEMBER?

CAN I HELP YOU?

I'M THE ONE WHO WAS OUT HERE LAST WEEK PICKING MUSHROOMS. I'M SHOWING MY PARTNER JASON AROUND THE YARD.

POOL
I KNEW YOUR FATHER WHEN HE FARMED THIS AREA.

WELL, THERE'S LOTS TO SEE— BESIDES THIS.
BUT YOU'RE NOT THE FIRST TO COME LOOKING.

DIDN'T THINK I'D HAVE TO PATROL MY PROPERTY.

SO YOU DON'T SEE A PROBLEM WITH PIPING OIL THROUGH FARMLAND?

AHAH! I KNEW IT.

WE'VE HAD PIPELINES FOR DECADES. HELL, YOUR DAD SAW THEM GO INTO THE GROUND!

YOU NEED OIL JUST AS MUCH AS THE REST OF US.
I SAW YOUR CAR OUT ON THE YARD.

I DON'T SEE THAT CHANGING ANY TIME SOON.

AND YOU CAN PROTEST ALL YOU WANT BUT AT THE END OF THE DAY IT'S UP TO THE MARKET.

WE DON'T NEED MORE PIPELINES.

BEFORE YOU KNOW IT THIS LAND WON'T BE FIT TO FARM ANY LONGER.

HEY NOW, LET'S REMEMBER WHOSE LAND YOU'RE ON.
POOL

YOU MAY HAVE GROWN UP HERE BUT YOU'RE STANDING ON MY PROPERTY.
SHOW SOME RESPECT.

YOUR PROPERTY, HER PROPERTY...

IT'S STILL STOLEN!

ENERGY COMPANIES WILL PAY OFF FARMERS AND BOAST ABOUT JOBS BUT THEY NEVER MENTION THE SPILLS, THE PROFIT MARGINS...

OR THE CRAP THEY LEAVE BEHIND.

I THINK IT'S TIME FOR YOU TWO TO BE ON YOUR WAY.
BARK!

WE WERE JUST THINKING THE SAME THING WEREN'T WE, JASON?

NO

WE'RE HERE TO SEE WHERE YOU GREW UP.

FINE.

BUT THIS PART OF THE FARM IS OFF LIMITS.

I CAN SHOW YOU THE OLD ORCHARD — THERE MIGHT STILL BE A FEW APPLE TREES LEFT.

THIS WAY

I THINK WE SHOULD GO – I FEEL KIND OF SICK BEING HERE.

I'M SORRY.
NO, IT'S MY FAULT.

BARK
BARK

YOU HAVEN'T TOLD ME ABOUT YOUR VISIT TO THE FARM YET JASON, WHAT DID YOU THINK OF IT?

UHH...

MOM, IT WAS AWFUL ...THE PEOPLE WHO LIVE THERE NOW...

BILL AND CINDY? THEY'RE GOOD PEOPLE. WHEN YOUR DAD DIED, THEY MADE THE TRANSITION REALLY EASY ON US. I'VE ALWAYS APPRECIATED THAT.

WELL, BILL BASICALLY TOLD US WE HAD TO GET OFF HIS PROPERTY.

YOU DON'T REALIZE HOW BAD IT IS, MOM! HE'S GOT A PIPELINE RUNNING RIGHT THROUGH THE FARM!

YOU'VE HEARD ABOUT IT?
OH... OF COURSE.

WELL, PETE AT CHURCH HAS BEEN BRINGING IT UP EVERY SUNDAY.

HE WAS ACTUALLY TRYING TO GET A GROUP TOGETHER FOR SOME SORT OF DEMONSTRATION, BUT NOTHING CAME OF IT.

IT HADN'T OCCURRED TO ME IT'S THE SAME PIPELINE THAT WAS INSTALLED WHEN WE WERE LIVING THERE.

I REMEMBER YOUR DAD WAS PRETTY CONFLICTED ABOUT IT.
HE'D INHERITED THE LAND FROM HIS FATHER.

BUT IT WAS JUST ME AND HIM—WE COULDN'T DO MUCH ABOUT IT, AND THE MONEY DID HELP.

THAT'S KIND OF THE MENTALITY OUT HERE ISN'T IT? EVERY MAN FOR HIMSELF.

OH NOT AT ALL! I'VE HEARD THAT PEOPLE IN THIS AREA DONATE MORE PER CAPITA THAN ANYWHERE ELSE IN THE COUNTRY.

AND WE LOOK OUT FOR EACH OTHER. THE FAMILY TIES GO BACK A LONG WAY.

BUT ONLY SO FAR.
RIGHT!

AND WE NEED TO BE BETTER NEIGHBOURS.

AND LEARN ABOUT OTHER CULTURES TOO!

...YEAH...

WE'LL TAKE CARE OF THE DISHES.
I DIDN'T EVEN OFFER YOU ANY COFFEE OR TEA.

WE'RE FINE, MOM.
THANKS FOR DINNER, KAREN.
OH YOU'RE SO WELCOME IT'S SUCH A TREAT TO HAVE YOU HERE.

I'M GOING TO SEE IF I CAN FIND SOME OLD FAMILY PHOTOS.
MOM, NO...

NOT SO FAST.

BEFORE WE HEAD BACK TO THE CITY, CAN WE MAKE A LITTLE DETOUR?
THERE'S A TRAIL NEAR THE SOUTH EDGE OF THE ESCARPMENT
I THINK WE CAN FIND IT.
THIS PLACE
I FEEL LIKE I KNOW IT.
LIKE IT KNOWS ME.

FREEDOM

LET'S GO THIS WAY.

SHOULDN'T BE MORE THAN ANOTHER FIFTEEN MINUTES.

NEED SOME WATER?

NAH, I'M GOOD.

I'M SAD WE DIDN'T COME OUT HERE MORE OFTEN THIS SUMMER.
I ALWAYS TOOK IT FOR GRANTED WHEN WE WERE AT THE BIBLE CAMP.

YEAH.

HOW'S WORK BEEN GOING?

ME TOO.

OH FINE.
WHO WAS THAT GIRL FROM PARK VALLEY THAT I MET – KATIE?
SHE SEEMS NICE.

YEAH, SHE'S GREAT.

MAYBE YOU SHOULD ASK HER OUT ON A DATE.

YOU FIND MORE SASKATOONS?
MAYBE.
YUP

COME ON. I'M BABY SITTING FOR YOUR SISTER TONIGHT.

WHICH ONE?
HEIDI. TRAVIS IS BACK ON THE ROAD AND SHE NEEDS A BREAK FROM THOSE KIDS.
CLICK
CHI-CHI

SERIOUSLY, THOUGH...

YOU'RE ALMOST 40.

YOU SHOULD BE GOING ON DATES.

REALLY? WE'RE DOING THIS NOW?

YOU'VE GOT AN APARTMENT, A CAR, A JOB...

YOU'RE ALMOST THERE...
AND WHERE IS THAT?

AT LEAST YOU'RE GOING TO A CHURCH WITH MORE YOUNG PEOPLE. MAYBE PASTOR MIKE COULD SET YOU UP WITH SOMEONE.
COME ON, MA. THAT WOULD BE SO INAPPROPRIATE.

CAN WE JUST LEAVE IT?

NA OBA, THOMAS...

I JUST THINK SOMEONE WOULD BE LUCKY TO HAVE YOU AS A HUSBAND.

THANKS FOR COMING ON THAT WALK WITH ME.
OF COURSE.

C posting...

Grateful for Creation today! #godhasaplan #blessed up #nature

PastorMike
God has blessed me with th
family I could imagine...
25 comments
TAP TAP

SCRATCH
SCRATCH

309

Activity
Gabby316 liked your photo
PastorMike liked your photo
RubyReimer liked your
EnnsJJ liked your

ONE FLAT WHITE TO GO.

COFFEE
DRIP 2
AMERICANO 3
LATTE 3.5
CAPPUCCINO 3.5
FLAT WHITE 4
MOCHA 3.5
NOT COFFEE
TEA 2.5
SPARKLING 2
THOMAS! HEY!

OH, HI KATIE.

I FEEL LIKE THIS IS THE FIRST TIME I'VE RUN INTO YOU OUTSIDE OF CHURCH.

HAHA ... ... YEAH HOW'S IT GOING?

THERE'S JUST SO MUCH OUTREACH HAPPENING NOW AND WE'RE STARTING TO PLAN ANOTHER MISSIONS TRIP.

I'VE BEEN SO BUSY LATELY WITH EVERYTHING. AND I KNOW GOD WANTS ME TO SLOW DOWN A BIT BUT I'M JUST SO EXCITED ABOUT ALL THE STUFF WE'RE PLANNING AT PARK VALLEY!
OH YEAH?

YOU KNOW, I'M JUST REALIZING THAT IT'S KIND OF PERFECT THAT I RAN INTO YOU! PASTOR MIKE PUT ME IN CHARGE OF FINDING YOUTH SPONSORS, AND IT'S BEEN REALLY CHALLENGING.

I WAS JUST PRAYING ABOUT IT, AND NOW HERE YOU ARE!

DIDN'T YOU USED TO WORK AT CAMP?

I DID, YEAH.

I'M SURE YOU'D MAKE AN AMAZING SPONSOR.
PROMISE ME YOU'LL AT LEAST PRAY ABOUT IT?
SURE.
liked by others
Valley Church
Alive for God MIX
New playlist to get your heart + soul ready for God. Link in bio. #parkvalley #worship #kingdommusic
HOURS
TAP
TAP

BUZZ

HI THOMAS, I WAS THINKING: YOU'RE OFF FROM WORK THIS WEEKEND...

YEAH.

AND LAST TIME YOU WERE OUT IT WAS SO BUSY WITH THE GRANDKIDS THAT YOUR PA DIDN'T GET TO VISIT WITH YOU.

UMHM.

WHY DON'T YOU COME FOR FASPA TOMORROW?
YEAH, OK.

AND COULD YOU GRAB SOME THINGS FROM FRIESEN'S ON YOUR WAY OUT? I NEED POTATOES AND ONIONS.
SURE.

FRIESEN'S
farms
OPEN

WELCOME!

CAMP

FAR OUT

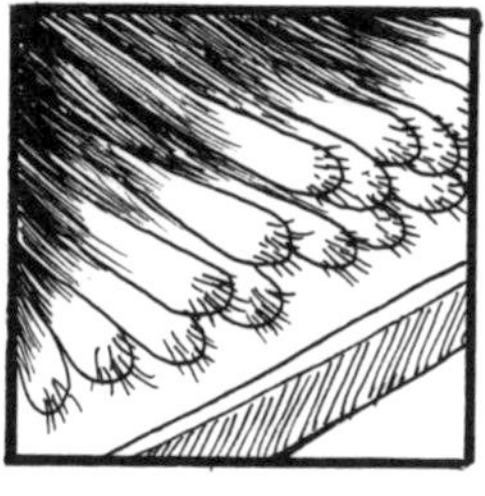

WHOOPS! PARDON ME.

BUMP
BUMP

JUST TRYING TO GET THESE ALL INSIDE BEFORE THE FROST HITS.
CAMP

FRESH TOMATOES.

YOU CAN'T BEAT 'EM.

IKE! GET OUT OF HERE. YOU'RE WEIRDING OUT THE CUSTOMERS.
FEST

HAHA, HE'S FINE.
YOU LIKE TOMATOES DON'T YOU?

...OF COURSE.

SOMETIMES SHE FORGETS WE'RE ON A FARM.

LAST I CHECKED THAT MEANS MORE FREEDOM, NOT LESS.

AFTER ALL THAT YOU'RE NOT EVEN GONNA BUY ANY TOMATOES?
CAMP

I'M KIDDING RELAX!
SORRY ABOUT MY BROTHER ISAAC.

IT'S FINE, THANK YOU!
CAMP

DID ANYONE WANT ANY DESSERT? SOME MATÉ?
CAMP

I'M GOOD THANKS.

YOUR MA TELLS ME YOU'VE STARTED DATING AGAIN.

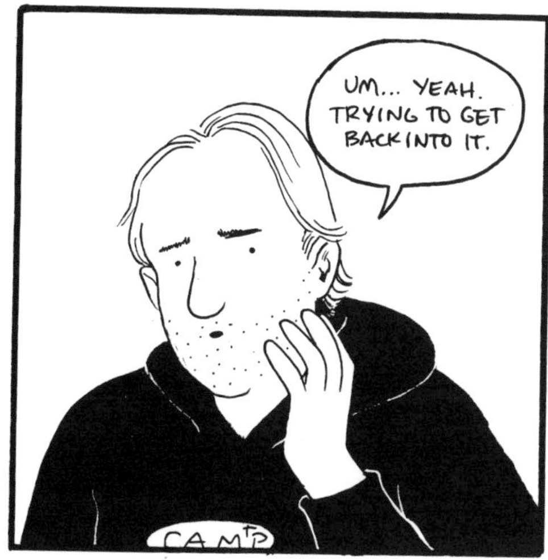
UM... YEAH. TRYING TO GET BACK INTO IT.
CAMP

I KNOW IT'S NOT EASY, ESPECIALLY AT YOUR AGE.
WE CONTINUE TO PRAY THAT YOU'LL FIND THE RIGHT GIRL.

GOD DIDN'T INTEND FOR MAN TO BE ALONE.

IT'S GOOD YOU'RE AT PARK VALLEY. THERE'S LOTS OF YOUNG PEOPLE THERE.
YOU JUST NEED TO TAKE SOME INITIATIVE.

ACTUALLY, I'M GOING TO BE A YOUTH SPONSOR FOR THEIR UPCOMING MISSION TRIP.

OBA! THAT'S WONDERFUL TO HEAR, SON!

I SHOULD PROBABLY GO. THERE'S A LOT OF WORK I HAVE TO DO, TO GET READY.
OF COURSE.

WHEN YOU SEE PRAEDJA MIKE PASS ALONG MY GREETINGS.

I'M ALWAYS THANKFUL WHEN I SEE A FULL CHURCH PARKING LOT.

CHI-CHI

TAP TAP TAP TAP TAP TAP
Hey Mike ☺ Just wanted to make sure you got my email about becoming a youth sponsor at Park Valley. I'm excited for the upcoming trip and I know God is to do great things through us.

seen

through us.
Hi Thomas, it's great to hear about your desire to contribute to Park Valley!
Unfortunately, we've filled all our open spots and no longer need youth sponsors. But there are other ways you can support the missions trip. I'll make sure to add your name to our email list.

TAP TAP TAP TAP

email list.
When I talked to Katie yesterday she said you were in desperate need of more sponsors...
I'm serious about going! I can be a real asset! I have experience from all my work with youth at camp.
I know God is calling me to serve in this way.
Katie even said I was an answer to prayer!

... Mike is typing

an answer to prayer
I'm sorry, Thomas
The Truth is that we have some members on our planning team who worked with you at camp.

at camp.
They have voiced concerns based on what you shared during a staff retreat. If it ever got out, the parents would hold Park Valley responsible. It could do a lot of damage.

damage.
You're still welcome at Park Valley!
Message...

VROOM!

MOTOR
INN
RESTAURANT & BAR

UH...

MGD, I GUESS.

CAMP

A RUM AND COKE FOR ME, AND ANOTHER OF WHATEVER HE'S HAVING.
CAMP

I HAVEN'T SEEN YOU HERE BEFORE.

I LIVE IN THE NEIGHBOURING TOWN.
JUST ON MY WAY HOME FROM DINNER WITH MY PARENTS.

SO YOU GREW UP AROUND HERE?
UNFORTUNATELY.
HA! NOT ME, BORN AND RAISED IN THE CITY.
CAMP

MY SISTER BOUGHT SOME LAND AROUND HERE A FEW YEARS AGO. I STARTED HELPING HER OUT HERE AND THERE... NOW I'M HOOKED!

SO YOU'RE NOT MENNONITE THEN?

I'VE GOT THE RIGHT LAST NAME, APPARENTLY. BUT I'M NOT, YOU KNOW, RELIGIOUS.

WHEN I WAS A KID MY PARENTS LEFT THEIR CHURCH AND STARTED A NEW ONE WITH SOME FRIENDS BUT IT DIDN'T LAST.

BUT GROWING UP IS HARD, NO MATTER WHERE YOU ARE.

I'M JUST GRATEFUL WE DIDN'T HAVE TO DO IT WITH THE INTERNET.

WHAT KIDS TODAY DO TO EACHOTHER ONLINE?— SHIT IS DARK.

SOMETIMES I FEEL A BIT, I DUNNO, JEALOUS?

LIKE, WE HAD TO SEARCH AND STRUGGLE TO FIND, YOU KNOW, ENTERTAINMENT AND COMMUNITY — BUT NOW IT'S ALL THERE WITHOUT ANY WORK.

BUT JUST THINK ABOUT HOW MUCH MORE THAT EFFORT MADE YOU APPRECIATE WHAT YOU FOUND.
I GUESS.

YOU'RE A BIT OF A WHINER, AREN'T YOU?

DON'T YOU EVER WONDER WHO YOU'D BE IF YOU WERE A TEENAGER TODAY?

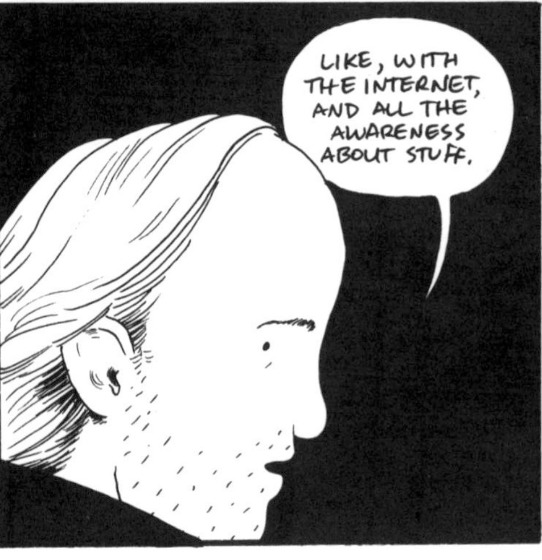
LIKE, WITH THE INTERNET, AND ALL THE AWARENESS ABOUT STUFF.

WITH MORE OPTIONS...

MORE FREEDOM.

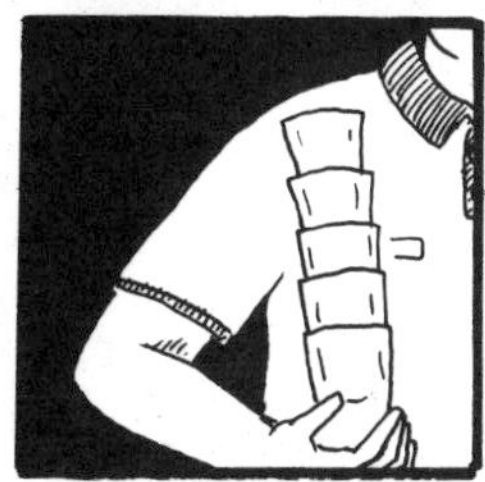

COME TO THINK OF IT I GUESS MY PARENTS SORT OF SAY THE SAME THING, HA HA... HOW WE'RE ALL SO MUCH BETTER OFF THAN THEY WERE.

AND YOU BELIEVE THEM?! HAHA, I'M KIDDING! WHEN I WAS GROWING UP, I NEVER HEARD THE END OF IT.

EVERY TIME I STEPPED OUT OF LINE I HAD TO HEAR ABOUT ALL THE SACRIFICES MY GRANDPARENTS MADE, AND THE SAC-RIFICES THEIR PARENTS MADE... BLAH BLAH BLAH...
LIKE, OK. BUT WASN'T PART OF THE GOAL TO GIVE THE NEXT GENERATION OPTIONS THEY DIDNT HAVE?
CAMP

WELL, FOR MY FAMILY IT WAS ALWAYS ABOUT THE FREEDOM TO PRACTICE THEIR FAITH. MY PARENTS GREW UP IN PARAGUAY, AND THEIR PARENTS BARELY MADE IT OUT OF RUSSIA ... I MEAN, UKRAINE.

MY DAD STILL TALKS ABOUT HOW GOD PROTECTED OUR FAMILY IN ORDER TO BRING US HERE.
IN SPITE OF EVERYTHING, THEY TRUSTED IN GOD, AND HE WAS ALWAYS FAITHFUL.

NO I GET IT... YOU'VE GOTTA RESPECT YOUR ELDERS...

BUT I KNEW WITH MINE WE WERE NEVER GONNA SEE EYE TO EYE.

SOUNDS LIKE YOU COULD USE A LITTLE DISTANCE FROM YOURS.

HEY, COME ON. I DIDN'T MEAN IT LIKE THAT.

CLAMP

I THINK I'M GONNA HEAD HOME.

I'VE GOT YOUR DRINK.
CAMP
IT'S FINE.

YOUR MONEY'S NO GOOD HERE.

Sept 19

COME ON, MAN.
I'M SORRY IF I WAS TOO FORWARD.

YOU SEEM LIKE A REALLY NICE GUY. I'D LIKE TO CHAT MORE.

I SHOULD REALLY GO HOME.

I, UH...

I'VE GOTTA WORK TOMORROW.

SORRY.

HEY I'M NOT TRYING TO PRESSURE YOU INTO ANYTHING.
CAMP

AT LEAST GIVE ME YOUR NUMBER!
YOUR NAME!
SLAM!

9:17
Park Valley Radio
Alive for God!

I WANT TO TOUCH YOU
I WANT TO SEE YOUR
I WANT

FACE
TO KNOW
I AM REACHIN
CAMP

YOU MU
FOR THE HIGHE

GOD, WHAT IS WRONG WITH ME?!

CA

SLAM!

NA? BACK FOR DESSERT?!

BREYER
Vanilla

FRIESEN'S
farm
CONTACT
SHARE

Hi, I'm Thomas
I put Customers FIRST
THE HOME
STOP
PARK VALLEY CHURCH
GOD IS AT WORK!
SERVICES
8:30 10AM 6PM

BETTER TIMES

SQUEAK-A
SQUEAK-A
SQUEAK-A

WOULD ERIC LIKE SOME TEA BEFORE BED?

HE'S OK, THANKS.
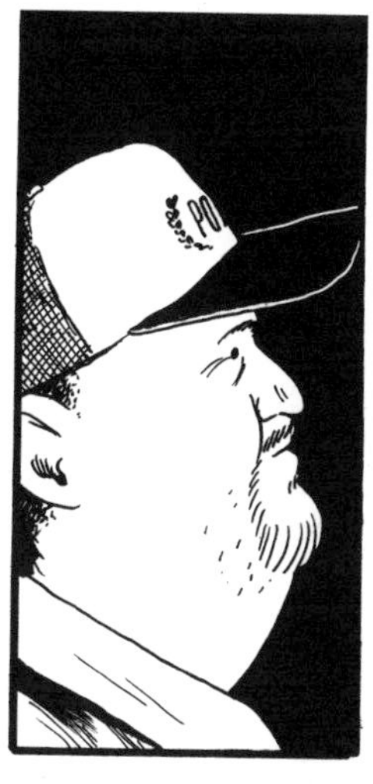

COME ON, BOYS! TIME FOR SCHOOL.

I SHOULD BE GOING. GOTTA MAKE AN EARLY START.

WILLIAM, LOOK OUT FOR YOUR BROTHER.
AND I DON'T WANT TO HEAR ANY COMPLAINING.

I'M A BIT LATE WITH THE HARVEST THIS YEAR.

YES, MA'AM

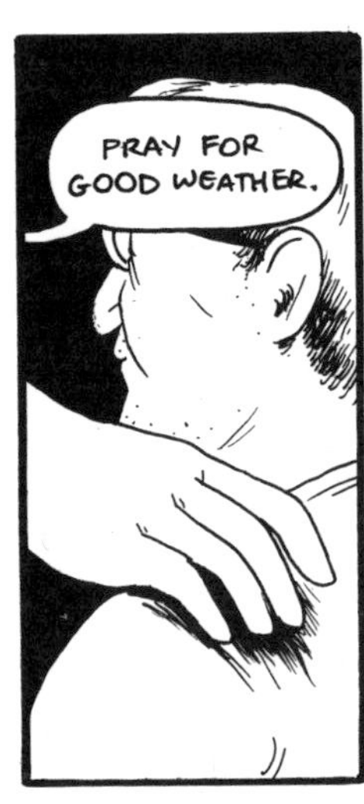
PRAY FOR GOOD WEATHER.

COME ON, ERIC!

CLICK

NO, IT'S BETTER TO SIT IN THE BACK.

ONLY LOSERS SIT UP AT THE FRONT.

BOP!

HEY!

HOW WAS ERIC TODAY?

OH, SAME AS USUAL.

RELAX KID! IT WAS JUST AN APPLE CORE.

WIMPS

YOU CAN... GO TO HELL!
OOOH. HAHA

DID YOU ASK THE NURSES ABOUT THE PIANO?

YEAH. HE ISN'T PLAYING IT.

THE NURSES REALLY SHOULD BE HELPING HIM.

WELL?

ARE YOU GOING TO DO SOMETHING ABOUT THAT?

SCRATCH
SCRATCH

LISTEN
SCRATCH

IF HE'S NOT GONNA PLAY IT, HE'S NOT GONNA PLAY IT.

THE NURSES HAVE OTHER THINGS TO WORRY ABOUT.

WHERE'S MY BOY, SCRAPPY?

THE PIANO WAS A WASTE OF MONEY, IF YOU ASK ME. HE'S FINE JUST WATCHING T.V.

YOU DON'T MEAN THAT, BILL.
SURE I DO.

YOUR DAD MADE SURE THAT YOUR BROTHER WOULD BE TAKEN CARE OF.

WE HAD TO SAVE FOR AL-MOST TWENTY YEARS TO BUY LAND. ALL BE-CAUSE ERIC HAD TO BE TAKEN CARE OF.

THAT'S VERY GOOD, ERIC.

WE COULD HAVE TAKEN HIM IN.

I LOVE HOW CASUALLY YOU CAN SAY THAT.

MOM! LOOK AT THIS!

WHEN I'D JUST END UP HAVING ANOTHER MAN TO LOOK AFTER.

OH, DON'T GET ALL DRAM-ATIC. I'M PRETTY LOW MAIN-TENANCE.

WILLIAM, WHY DON'T YOU GO SEE IF YOUR FATHER NEEDS SOME HELP IN THE SHOP?

GOOD TIMING!

ESPECIALLY COMPARED TO YOUR DAD.
HAH!

ZZZZ

GRAB A BROOM.

I BETTER GET TO BED. I PROMISED DEB THAT I'D HELP TIE COMFORTERS WITH HER TOMOR-ROW AT BMF.

DON'T STAY UP TOO LATE.

YOU'VE GOT AN EARLY MORNING TOO.

I JUST... I REMEMBER HIM

PLAYING IT WHEN WE WERE ALL YOUNGER.

HE WAS LIKE A DIFFERENT PERSON.

I HATE KNOWING THAT THINGS COULD BE BETTER FOR HIM, BUT NOT BEING ABLE TO DO ANYTHING ABOUT IT.

IT'S YOUR IDEA OF BETTER.

MAYBE IT MAKES NO DIFFERENCE TO HIM.
PAT
PAT

MAYBE.
CLICK
GOOD NIGHT.

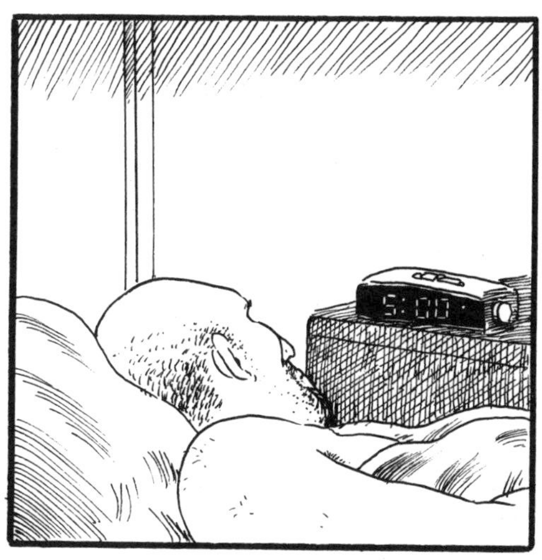
5:00

HI DEB, YES, ON MY WAY NOW. I'LL SEE YOU SOON.

ENTRANCE

BILL MUST BE CLOSE TO FINISHED HARVESTING.
ALMOST!

WE'RE COUNTING DOWN THE DAYS UNTIL MEXICO.

YOU SHOULD COME WITH US SOME TIME.

REALLY HELPS GET US THROUGH THE WINTER.

WE BOTH HAVE RELATIVES IN THE COLONIES DOWN THERE, OBA...

NA, ABE WOULD NEVER GO FOR IT.

AH, ABE... EVER THE MORAL AUTHORITY.

SOMETIMES I THINK THAT MAN JUST WANTS EVERY-ONE TO SUFFER.

I CAN FEEL HIM JUDGING ME AND HE'S NOT EVEN HERE.
HAHA

NOBODY SHOULD EVER FLY ANYWHERE.
WE SHOULD ALL BE HAVING A...

WHAT'S IT CALLED AGAIN?

A STAY-CATION?

YEAH, LET'S DRIVE OUR TRUCKS IN CIRCLES AT FORTY BELOW. HA HA HA!

OH, HE'D PROBABLY LIKE YOU TO THINK IT'S BECAUSE HE'S MORALLY CONSISTENT.

BUT IT'S ALSO BECAUSE WE'RE A BIT CHEAP. AND THE KIDS NEED US NEARBY.

THAT WAY OF THINKING... IT JUST DRIVES ME UP THE WALL.

IT GETS YOU NOWHERE AND IT HELPS NO ONE.
I DON'T DISAGREE.
WE'RE HARDLY MARTYRS.

BUT I'VE ALWAYS LIKED THAT EXPRESSION...

BLOOM WHERE YOU'RE PLANTED.

DID YOU FORGET WHO YOU'RE TALKING TO?
I'VE GOT THAT CROSS STITCH HANGING ON MY WALL!

HMPH!

HA HA HA
HE HE HE

SO, THE KIDS AND GRANDKIDS ARE ALL DOING WELL? HOW IS THOMAS? STILL AT THE HOME DEPOT?

THEY'RE ALL PRETTY GOOD. THOMAS TOO.
I THINK A LOT OF IT HAS TO DO WITH PARK VALLEY.

HE TOLD US THE OTHER NIGHT THAT HE'S GOING TO BECOME A YOUTH SPONSOR, WHICH IS GOING TO BE SO GOOD FOR HIM.

I THINK HE STILL MISSES WORKING AT CAMP.

DOES IT BOTHER ABE THAT HIS SON IS GOING TO A DIFFERENT CHURCH?
SNIP

YES... BUT OUR DAUGHTERS' FAMILIES ALL GO TO DIFFERENT CHURCHES NOW TOO.
THOMAS WAS THE HOLDOUT... AND HE NEEDED A CHANGE.
HE JUST SEEMS SO LONELY.

HE'LL FIND SOME-ONE, DEB.

ALL DONE.
I'LL GRAB THE NEXT ONE.

YOU KNOW, I'VE BEEN WANTING TO CHECK OUT PARK VALLEY- I THINK BILL MIGHT LIKE IT... I HEARD THEY EVEN HAVE A CAFÉ!
YES, IT'S QUITE SOME-THING.

SPEAKING OF BILL, YOU SHOULD HAVE SEEN HIM A FEW WEEKS AGO.

I WAS WORRIED HE WAS GOING TO DO SOMETHING STUPID.

THERE WERE THESE KIDS ON THE FARM SNEAKING AROUND LOOKING AT THE PIPELINE THEY'RE REPLACING.

THANK GOD THAT'S ALMOST OVER.

WELL, IF YOU AGREE TO THAT PRICE I GUESS IT'S A DONE DEAL.

ANYWAY, ONE OF THEM GREW UP ON THE YARD, LONG BEFORE WE GOT THERE.
BILL SAYS HE KNEW HER FATHER.

AND THEY WERE YELLING ALL ABOUT STOLEN LAND AND GLOBAL WARMING AND ALL THAT, GETTING REALLY AGRESSIVE.

I'M DOING THIS FOR YOU AND YOUR BROTHER.

WITH YOUR MOM GONE, I DON'T HAVE TIME TO TAKE CARE OF YOU AND RUN THE FARM.

THAT SOMEONE WOULD COME AND SAY THAT ON YOUR OWN YARD, AFTER ALL YOU'VE INVESTED IN THAT FARM.

YOU REALLY TURNED THAT PLACE AROUND

I CAN DO MORE TO HELP!
I'M NO GOOD AT SCHOOL ANYWAY!

I'M STAYING HERE!

THESE YOUNG PEOPLE DON'T APPRECIATE THAT.
HOW COULD THEY?

DO YOU THINK ABOUT WHAT YOU'LL DO WITH THE FARM WHEN YOU'RE TOO OLD TO KEEP IT UP?

WHO KNOWS? MAYBE ONE DAY YOU'LL BE ABLE TO BUY YOUR OWN LAND,
BE YOUR OWN MAN.

OH, I SUPPOSE WE'LL RENT IT OUT OR SELL IT TO SOMEBODY.

IT'S GOOD LAND.

WE SHOULD BE ABLE TO GET A DECENT PRICE.

I'M AUCTIONING OFF EVERYTHING BEFORE WE MOVE TO TOWN, BUT I THOUGHT YOU'D WANT TO KEEP YOUR MOM'S SHEET MUSIC.

1 Missed call
1 Voice Mail

Z Z Z Z

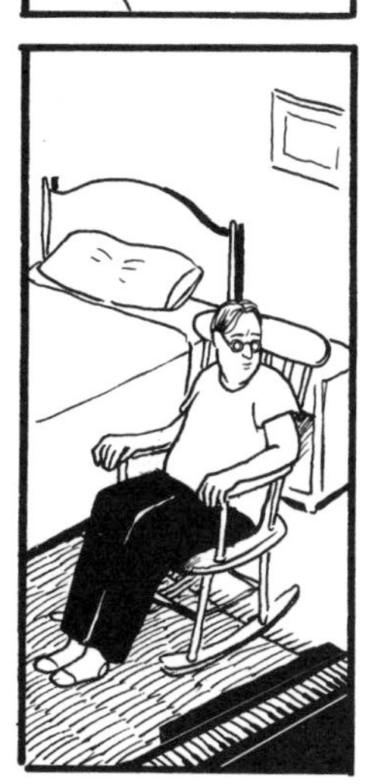

DEB AND I DECIDED TO GO FOR DINNER, SINCE BOTH OUR MEN ARE BUSY TONIGHT. THERE'S STILL SOME OF YESTERDAY'S CHICKEN AND RICE IN THE FRIDGE.

I DON'T UNDERSTAND WHY HE CAN'T JUST MOVE IN WITH US. WE COULD REALLY USE THE EXTRA MONEY.

YOUR FATHER SET ASIDE THAT MONEY FOR ERIC.
BUT WHY DIDN'T HE SET ASIDE ANYTHING FOR US?

YAMAHA

EVERY WEEK, WE HAVE DIFFERENT CHURCH GROUPS COME AND LEAD WORSHIP FOR OUR RESIDENTS.
OH, THAT'S PERFECT. ERIC LOVES MUSIC.

CLICK
YAMAH

PING
YAMAH

Pfffft

YOU'RE LUCKY, ERIC. DAD SECURED A SPOT FOR YOU AT THE CARE HOME IN TOWN. DON'T WORRY, WE'LL HELP MOVE YOU.
IT'S LIKE HE'S NEVER THROWN ANYTHING OUT.
Piano Pieces for Beginners
PIANO CLASSICS
PIANO CON

THRIFT SHOP
DROP OFF
WE CAN'T
TAKE IT A

IT'S TIME FOR OUR SUNDAY SERVICE.

IVE THANKS FORTOD
OUR SCRIPTURE FOR TODAY IS FROM PSALM 4.

ABE REIMER, FROM BIBLE MENNONITE FELLOWSHIP WILL BE SPEAKING.

ANSWER ME WHEN I CALL, OH GOD, DEFENDER OF MY CAUSE.

YOU SET ME FREE WHEN I AM HARD-PRESSED; HAVE MERCY ON ME AND HEAR MY PRAYER.

"YOU MORTALS, HOW LONG WILL YOU DISHONOUR MY GLORY HOW LONG WILL YOU WORSHIP DUMB IDOLS AND RUN AFTER FALSE GODS?"

KNOW THAT THE LORD DOES WONDERS FOR THE FAITHFUL; WHEN I CALL UPON THE LORD HE WILL HEAR ME.
TREMBLE, THEN, AND DO NOT SIN;
SPEAK TO YOUR HEART IN SILENCE UPON YOUR BED.

GIVE THANKS FOR T
OFFER THE APPOINTED SACRIFICES AND PUT YOUR TRUST IN THE LORD.
COUGH
COUGH
MANY ARE SAYING, "OH THAT WE MIGHT SEE BETTER TIMES!"

LIFT UP THE LIGHT OF YOUR COUNTENANCE UPON US, O LORD,

YOU HAVE PUT GLADNESS IN MY HEART, MORE THAN WHEN GRAIN AND WINE AND OIL INCREASE.

I LIE DOWN IN PEACE, AT ONCE I FALL ASLEEP;
FOR ONLY YOU, LORD, MAKE ME DWELL IN SAFETY.

HEAVEN

PARK VALLEY CHURCH
MISSIONS TRIP FUNDRAISER - FEB. 1
YOUTH AND YOUNG ADULT CLUBS - WEDNESDAYS AT 7PM

I DUNNO. IT'S JUST NICE TO BE IN A SPACE WHERE PEOPLE ARE SO POSITIVE AND SUPPORTIVE.

BUT ALSO...

REAL.

I GUESS THAT MAKES SENSE.

IT SEEMS REALLY DIFFERENT FROM THAT CHURCH YOUR PARENTS GO TO.
I CAN SEE WHY YOU STOPPED GOING.

YEAH, I'M GETTING BORED JUST THINKING ABOUT IT. THE HYMNS AT JUBILEE WOULD GO ON AND ON.

THE MUSIC AT PARK VALLEY IS REALLY GOOD. I THINK YOU'D LIKE IT!

YOU KNOW THEY'RE JUST AFTER YOUR MONEY, RIGHT?

YOU HAVEN'T EVEN STEPPED FOOT IN THE BUILDING.

LARISSA, YOU DIDN'T GROW UP AROUND THIS STUFF LIKE I DID. IT'S ALL THE SAME.

THAT'S WHY YOU NEED TO COME! IT'S NOT THE SAME AT ALL.

THE ONLY CHURCH YOU'VE EVER GONE TO WAS STUCK IN THE PAST.
PARK VALLEY IS DIFFERENT.

PASTOR MIKE TALKS ABOUT HOW CHURCHES NEED TO BE IN THE SPIRIT TO STAY RELEVANT.

CAN YOU NOT CALL HIM THAT?

IT'S CREEPY.

YOU'RE REALLY GETTING SERIOUS ABOUT THIS CHURCH STUFF, HEY?

BEFORE YOU LEAVE COULD YOU CLOSE THE BLINDS?

FINE, BUT CAN YOU TAKE OUT THE GARBAGE? I HAVE TO RUN - THE YOUTH MENTORS ARE MEETING TO PLAN FOR OUR MISSIONS TRIP.

AND FATHER, WE PRAY THAT YOU WOULD GUIDE OUR CONVERSATION AS WE PLAN THIS TRIP.
MAY EACH ONE OF THESE MENTORS FEEL YOUR HAND UPON THEM AS THEY PREPARE FOR THEIR IMPORTANT KINGDOM-BUILDING WORK.
AND IN THE NAME OF JESUS, ALL THE PEOPLE SAID...
AMEN!

BEING PART OF GOD'S KINGDOM MIGHT MAKE YOU SEEM STRANGE TO PEOPLE, ESPECIALLY IF THEY HAVENT OPENED THEMSELVES UP TO GOD'S LOVE.

BUT WE KNOW THAT LIVING IN THE TRUTH IS ACTUALLY LIKE HAVING A SUPERPOWER!

IT'S INCREDIBLY IMPORTANT FOR OUR YOUTH TO HAVE GOOD ROLE MODELS.

ESPECIALLY IN A CROSS-CULTURAL SETTING.

SO CAN ANYONE HERE REMIND ME WHY WE'RE DOING THIS MISSIONS TRIP?

TO BUILD A CHURCH FOR THE COMMUNITY WE'VE BEEN SUPPORTING IN ENSENADA!
WOOH!
WOOH!
CLAP

TO SHOW THEM HOW MUCH GOD LOVES THEM!
WOOOOOOH!
CLAP

AND LAST BUT NOT LEAST: TO GROW IN OUR FAITH!

SO WE'RE COLLECTING PLEDGES FOR THE MISSIONS TRIP AND I SIGNED US UP FOR $300. THINK IT'S OK IF I ASK YOUR PARENTS?
WHAT?!
IT'S FINE, I'LL PAY IT. BUT THERE'S ANOTHER THING...

TO BE A YOUTH MENTOR I HAVE TO SIGN THIS FORM...

COMMITTING TO CELIBACY OUTSIDE OF MARRIAGE.
WHAT?!

I MEAN, I'M NOT SURPRISED THEY HAVE ONE OF THOSE LIFESTYLE THINGS, BUT DOESN'T EVERY-BODY JUST LIE ABOUT IT?
I CAN'T DO THAT.

WHAT IS THIS TRIP EVEN FOR?! I DON'T GET WHY YOU'RE SUDDENLY SO INTO THIS?

I TOLD YOU! WE'RE GOING TO BUILD A CHURCH FOR A SMALL COMMUNITY IN MEXICO!
IF YOU CARE SO MUCH, WHY WOULDN'T YOU JUST SEND MONEY FOR THEM TO BUILD THEIR OWN CHURCH?

BECAUSE IT'S ABOUT MORE THAN THAT — IT'S IMPORTANT TO SEE WHAT LIFE IS LIKE IN OTHER PARTS OF THE WORLD — TO BUILD RELATIONSHIPS.
HAHA. WOW.

IT SOUNDS LIKE A BUNCH OF PRIVILEGED WHITE PEOPLE WHO JUST WANT TO FEEL GOOD ABOUT THEIR WINTER VACATION.

IT'S NOT JUST WHITE PEOPLE. ACTUALLY, THE GROUP IS PRETTY DIVERSE. AND WE'RE LEARNING SOME SPANISH FROM ONE OF THE OTHER MENTORS—HER FAMILY IS FROM MEXICO!
THAT DOESN'T MAKE THIS ANY LESS CRAZY.

DEREK, ALL YOU EVER DO IS SMOKE WEED AND BRO OUT WITH YOUR VIDEO GAMES. IT'S PATHETIC.
AT LEAST THIS CHURCH IS DOING SOMETHING TO HELP PEOPLE.

IF YOU'RE NOT GOING TO SUPPORT ME, THEN I DON'T KNOW IF WE SHOULD BE TOGETHER.

YOU KNOW, I WAS THINKING THE SAME THING.

I THOUGHT YOU WERE SMARTER THAN THIS.

YOU ARE SO FUCKING SELFISH.

SLAM!

SNIFF

YOU DID THE RIGHT THING.

HOW IS THAT IDIOT GOING TO TAKE CARE OF HIMSELF? I FEEL SO GUILTY...
BUT ALSO RELIEVED?

WHAT YOU FEEL IS VALID. YOU'RE LETTING GO OF THE BURDEN OF SIN.

I HAVE A MEETING COMING UP RIGHT AWAY, BUT I WANTED TO LET YOU KNOW WE HAVE A SUPPORT GROUP FOR SINGLES THAT GETS TOGETHER ON FRIDAYS. I THINK IT COULD BE REALLY GOOD FOR YOU.

LOADING

PLEASE STAY AND JOIN US FOR LUNCH!
THE BUILDING CREW IS JUST WRAPPING UP.
LARISSA, CAN YOU MAKE SURE THIS GETS CHARGED TO THE RIGHT ACCOUNT?
SURE THING!
HI- EXCUSE ME - AHEM PERDONEME ¿PUEDO PAGAR... LA COMIDA?
I CAN HELP YOU.

WOW! YOUR ENGLISH IS REALLY GOOD!

MY SPANISH IS TERRIBLE HAHAHA.
GATHER ROUND EVERYONE AND GET SOMETHING TO EAT. CATERERS TOO! WE'VE ORDERED MORE THAN ENOUGH!

THANKS TO PASTOR OSCAR FOR SHARING THAT BLESSING AND OFFERING THANKS FOR THE FOOD.

HE'S GOING TO STICK AROUND —RIGHT OSCAR? HEH HEH... TO HELP WITH TRANSLATION.

PRAISE GOD FOR KEEPING US SAFE AND DILIGENT IN OUR WORK! WE HAVE FAITH THAT THIS CHURCH WILL BE A TESTAMENT TO HIS GLORY.

WE CAME HERE BECAUSE WE LOVE GOD... AND GOD LOVES YOU.

BEFORE WE HEAD BACK TO CANADA, I WANT TO LEAVE YOU WITH A TRUTH MORE STABLE AND RELIABLE THAN ANY BUILDING.

MORE VALUABLE THAN ANY EARTHLY RICHES.

SALVATION IS FREE TO ALL WHO ACCEPT JESUS CHRIST AS THEIR SAVIOUR.

WITH HIS DEATH ON THE CROSS, JESUS BOUGHT US EACH A PLACE IN HEAVEN.

IT'S NOT SOMETHING YOU CAN EARN, AND JUST BEING A GOOD PERSON ISN'T ENOUGH.

THIS IS WHAT WE MEAN WHEN WE TALK ABOUT BEING SAVED BY GRACE.

WHAT IS GRACE? ANYONE CARE TO SHARE? LARISSA?

UM...

I GUESS IT'S LIKE... WHEN YOU'VE REALLY HURT SOMEONE YOU CARE ABOUT, AND IT'S SO BAD YOU CAN'T EVEN TELL THEM YOU'RE SORRY BECAUSE IT WOULD JUST MAKE THINGS WORSE.

AND GRACE IS LIKE THAT PERSON TELLING YOU IT'S OK. NOT WHAT YOU DID, BUT THAT YOU'RE OK... FORGIVENESS WHEN IT SEEMS IMPOSSIBLE.
AMEN.
THAT'S SO WELL-PUT, LARISSA.
JESUS PULLED OFF THE IMPOSSIBLE – HE TOOK ON EVERY HUMAN SIN – EVEN THE ONES THAT HAVEN'T HAPPENED YET, AND HE SAID YOU'RE OK.
IN FACT, HE SAYS WE'RE MORE THAN OK!
WE ARE LOVED AND CHOSEN BY GOD TO JOIN HIM FOR ETERNITY.
OUR WORLD IS SO BROKEN AND WE ARE ALL HURTING.
PART OF THE GOOD NEWS IS KNOWING THAT THIS WORLD IS PASSING AWAY.
THAT'S WHY IT'S SO IMPORTANT TO KEEP OUR ATTENTION ON HEAVEN AND FOCUS ON ETERNAL REWARDS RATHER THAN EARTHLY RICHES.

WE'VE SEEN THE BEAUTY OF CREATION DURING OUR TIME HERE.
HEAVEN WILL BE MORE BRILLIANT THAN ANY OF US CAN IMAGINE.
BUT IT PALES IN COMPARISON TO WHAT'S IN STORE FOR GOD'S PEOPLE.
THIS LIFE IS ONLY A SPLIT SECOND COMPARED TO ETERNITY BUT EVERY-THING DEPENDS ON IT.
MENTORS PLEASE COME FOR-WARD.

I INVITE YOU TO COME FORWARD NOW AND COMMIT TO FOLLOWING JESUS FROM THIS DAY TO THE END OF DAYS.

OUR MENTORS ARE STANDING BY TO PRAY WITH YOU, IF YOU FEEL GOD PULLING AT YOUR HEART.

YOU MIGHT NOT HEAR HIS VOICE RIGHT AWAY.
IT MIGHT BE VERY QUIET.
BETTER

IS ONE DAY IN YOUR

COURTS THAN THOUSANDS ELSEWHERE...

HI AGAIN! MY NAME IS LARISSA, AND YOU ARE...
JUAN.

DEAR GOD, THANK YOU FOR JUAN AND FOR HIS DECISION TO DEDICATE HIS LIFE TO YOU TOD—
I LIKED YOUR SPEECH, LARISSA.

UM, THANKS. I HOPE—
I COULD TELL IT WAS FROM THE HEART.

EXCUSE ME FOR INTERRUPTING YOUR PRAYER.
I-

I HOPE YOU GOT WHAT YOU CAME FOR.

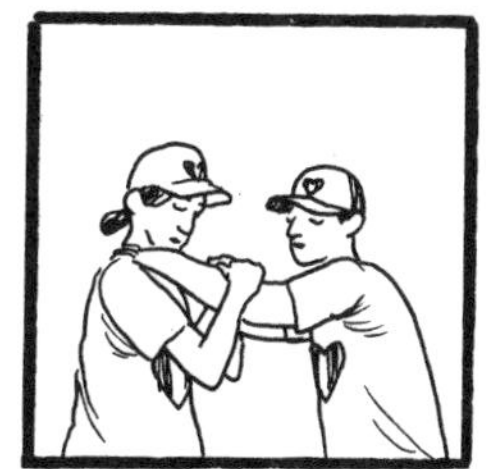

I HATE TO INTERRUPT BUT WE DO NEED TO GET GOING. OSCAR AND I WILL CLOSE WITH A PRAYER IN A MOMENT.

... FOR EVER AND EVER, AMEN. BLESSINGS TO YOU, OSCAR, AND TO YOUR CONGREGATION AS YOU CARRY ON GOD'S WORK FOR YOUR BROTHERS AND SISTERS HERE IN ENSENADA.
PRAISE GOD YOU COULD BE HERE WITH US. WE WILL BE PRAYING FOR YOU AND YOUR CHURCH IN CANADA.

READY TO GO, LARISSA?

THAT WAS SOME GREAT SHARING TODAY. I HOPE YOU KNOW HOW IMPORTANT YOU WERE TO OUR WORK HERE.
NO DOUBT YOU WON SOME SOULS FOR GOD.
ARE WE JUST... LEAVING THE CHURCH UNFINISHED?
WELL, YES. WE COULD ONLY STAY FOR A WEEK. AND THE PEOPLE HERE NEED TO TAKE OWNERSHIP OF THE PROJECT. THIS TRIP WAS ABOUT SO MUCH MORE THAN A BUILDING.
BUT YOU'RE RIGHT. WE SHOULD ALWAYS STRIVE TO DO BETTER.
I HOPE YOU SERIOUSLY CONSIDER ENROLLING IN OUR MINISTRY TRAINING PROGRAM. I SEE SO MUCH POTENTIAL IN YOU.
ME? REALLY?

COULD YOU CLOSE THE BLIND?

WHAT GAME ARE YOU PLAYING?

OH, IT'S JUST AN OLD ZELDA - I'VE ALREADY BEAT IT A FEW TIMES.

YOU MUST BE LOOKING FORWARD TO GETTING BACK.

YEAH, DEFINITELY!

SEEING YOUR FRIENDS AND FAMILY.

I BET YOU MISS YOUR PARENTS.

YEAH MY DAD SAID IF I WENT ON THIS TRIP HE'D GET ME ANY GAME I WANTED.

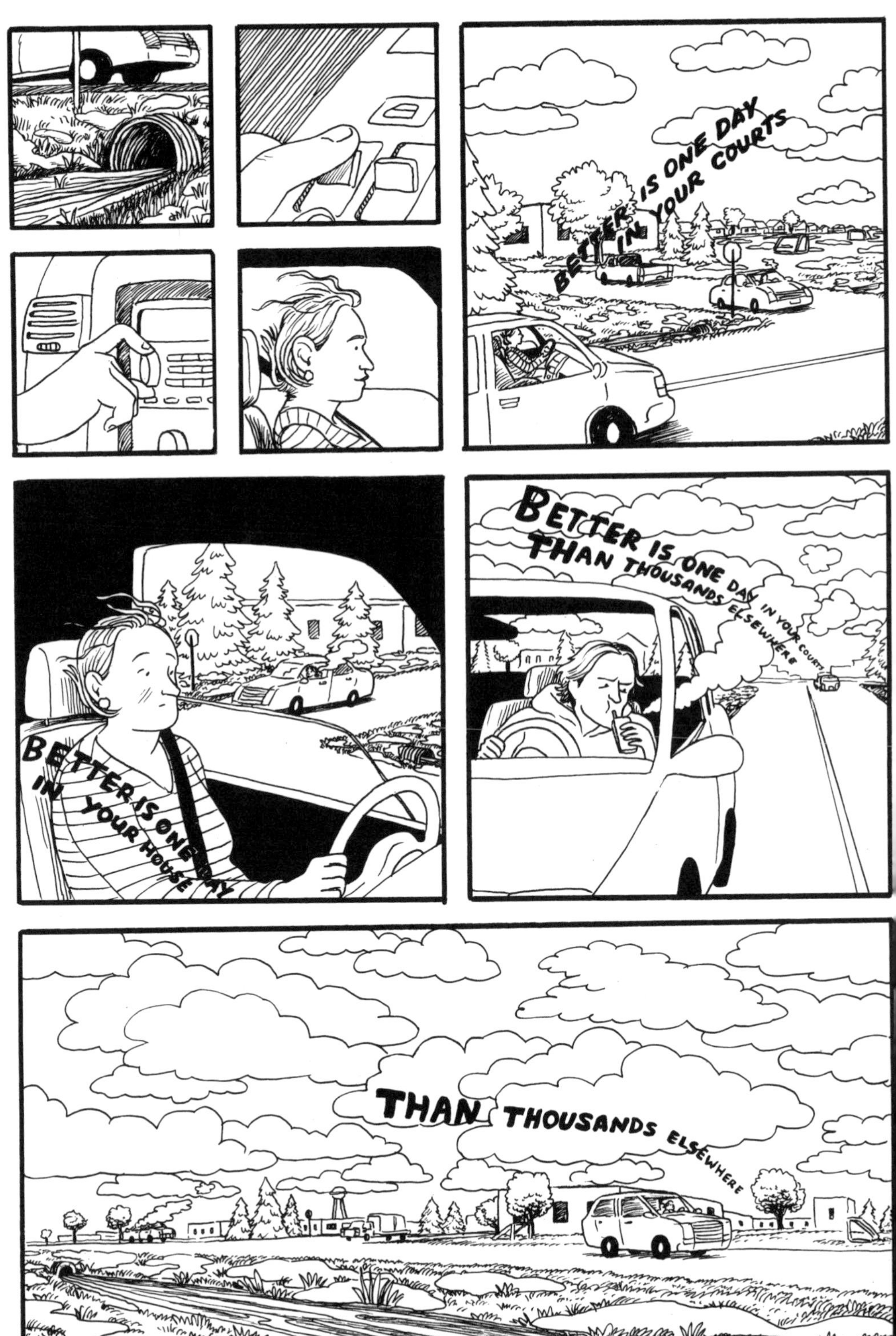
BETTER IS ONE DAY
IN YOUR COURTS
BETTER IS ONE DAY
IN YOUR HOUSE
BETTER IS ONE DAY IN YOUR COURTS
THAN THOUSANDS ELSEWHERE
THAN THOUSANDS ELSEWHERE

BETTERTIMES II

FRIESEN
farm stock
WELCOME

I THINK WE'RE GONNA NEED TO REPLACE THIS DOORKNOB.

WELCOME

I THINK WE'RE GONNA NEED TO REPLACE THE DOOR KNOB!

WHAT?

I SAID: I THINK WE'RE GOING TO NEED TO REPLACE THE DOORKNOB!!!
OK. JEEZ.

I'M GONNA HEAD TO TOWN AND GET A NEW ONE. ANY-THING ELSE WE NEED?
SEE IF YOU CAN FIND SOME OF THAT PLASTIC FENCING — FOR DEER.

AND MAYBE A COUPLE EXTRA TARPS.

HEY MAN!

HEY.

I DIDN'T KNOW YOU WORKED HERE.
OH, YEAH. HAHA.

HEY, UM, SORRY ABOUT THAT NIGHT ... BACK IN THE FALL...
IT FEELS LIKE A LONG TIME AGO.

I MEANT TO COME BY YOUR SHOP AGAIN, AT SOME POINT.

BUT WINTER CAME AND THERE WAS SOME STUFF I HAD TO DEAL WITH, STUFF I'D BEEN AVOIDING.

THINGS ARE BETTER NOW BUT I'M STILL NOT GREAT AT FOLLOWING THROUGH.

IT'S ALL GOOD, MAN. I APPREC-IATE HEARING THAT, THOUGH.

SO... HOW LONG HAVE YOU BEEN WORKING HERE?

AH, IT'S BEEN A FEW YEARS NOW. I USED TO WORK AT CAMP EVERY SUMMER.

PROBABLY STUCK AROUND THERE A BIT TOO LONG... HEHE.

THO-MAS! THO-MAS!
DON'T YOU FIND HIM A BIT CREEPY? HE'S BEEN WORKING HERE, LIKE, FOREVER.

THOUGHT MAYBE I'D BECOME THE DIRECTOR ONE DAY, BUT IT DIDN'T WORK OUT THAT WAY.

ARE YOU TALKING ABOUT THE SAME CAMP THAT'S DOWN THE ROAD FROM OUR FARM?

YUP, THAT'S THE ONE.

IT'S ONE OF THOSE RELIGIOUS CAMPS, RIGHT?

STAFF

YEAH, IT WAS STARTED BY A FEW CHURCHES IN THE AREA, IN THE SEVENTIES.

ST

MY MOM USED TO VOL-UNTEER IN THE KITCHEN, SO WE ALWAYS SPENT OUR SUMMERS THERE.

MAN, WHAT'S YOUR PROBLEM? WHY ARE YOU ALWAYS STARING AT ME?
I'M NOT!

SEEMS LIKE WE BOTH ENJOY THE OUTDOORS!

YEAH
IT'S TOO BAD THERE ISN'T MUCH OUT HERE BESIDES FARMLAND.

WELL, IF YOU DRIVE WEST, PAST THE NEXT TOWN OVER, THERE ARE SOME AMAZING TRAILS AROUND THE ESCARPMENT.

I COULD SHOW YOU SOMETIME.

!

THOMAS! HEY! I THOUGHT I MIGHT SEE YOU HERE.

JUST CAME BY TO GRAB SOME ZIP TIES.

HEY, DON'T YOU HAVE THAT NEW ORGANIC FARM OFF HIGHWAY 24?
YEAH — FRIESEN'S. IT'S REALLY MY SISTER'S THING, THOUGH.

AND WHAT'S YOUR... UH, CONNECTION TO THOMAS?

ACTUALLY WE'RE JUST GETTING TO KNOW EACH OTHER.

THOMAS CAN'T HIDE AT HOME DEPOT FOREVER.

NAME'S IKE.
BILL

I LIKE THIS GUY...
AND I LIKE YOUR HAT!

HEHE. WELL YOU BOYS FEEL FREE TO DROP BY THE FARM ANYTIME, IF YOU EVER WANT A TOUR.

I ALWAYS KEEP A FEW COLD ONES IN THE FRIDGE.

SAY HI TO YOUR FOLKS!

REMEMBER THAT GUY I MET AT RUDY'S, LIKE SIX MONTHS AGO, THE ONE WHO CAME BY THE SHOP THAT ONE TIME?

YEAH, I THINK SO. INCREDIBLY SHY—NOT YOUR TYPE AT ALL. WHY?

WELL, MAYBE I DIDN'T PLAY IT SO WRONG AFTER ALL.

TURNS OUT HE WORKS AT HOME DEPOT. I FINALLY GOT HIS NUMBER!

I THOUGHT YOU SWORE OFF DATING REPRESSED MENNONITES.

HAHA, WELL OUT HERE WHAT OTHER OPTION DO I HAVE?

SINCE THIS IS OUR LAST NIGHT TOGETHER, WE'RE GOING TO TAKE TURNS SHARING SOMETHING GOD HAS TAUGHT US THIS SUMMER.
STAFF

OH, BY THE WAY, WHILE YOU WERE GONE SOMEONE CAME AND ASKED TO PUT UP SOME CAMP POSTERS IN THE SHOP.

DID YOU LET THEM?

GRAB A STICK FROM THE PILE, AND ONCE YOU'VE SHARED, YOU CAN TOSS IT INTO THE FIRE.

WHAT ELSE COULD I DO?

BESIDES, WE NEED TO FIT INTO THE COMMUNITY A BIT MORE.

...SO I GUESS WHAT I'M SAYING IS... I'VE HAD A LOT OF GREAT EXPERIENCES HERE... BUT THIS IS GOING TO BE MY LAST SUMMER.

YEAH, I GET THAT IT'S FOR THE SAKE OF THE BUSINESS...

BUT I'M NOT OUT HERE TO FIT INTO ANY-ONE'S MOULD.

I'M NOT SURE WHERE I'LL END UP, BUT I KNOW GOD IS CALLING ME SOMEWHERE ELSE.

HAH! OK THEN! LET'S CALL IT A DAY AND HIT THE BAR.

WHY DON'T YOU INVITE YOUR NEW FRIEND?
MAYBE

ALRIGHT! EVERY ONE CAN HEAD BACK TO THEIR CABINS.

THOMAS, CAN YOU HOLD ON?
STAF

I DOUBT HE'D WANT TO MEET THERE AGAIN, AFTER WHAT HAPPENED LAST TIME.

THESE ARE FROM THE GUYS SITTING AT THE BAR.

FROM ONE FARMER TO ANOTHER!

CHEERS!
K, BUT AFTER THIS ONE OF US HAS TO TAKE IT EASY ON THE DRINKS.

MORE ROOM AT THE BAR!

SO I CAN LISTEN TO THEM BITCH ABOUT TAXES AND TRUDEAU?

HAH! YEAH, RIGHT!

WHILE THEY'RE SITTING PRETTY UP THERE ON THEIR COMBINES I'M ON MY KNEES IN THE DIRT.

HEY, WEREN'T YOU THE ONE WHO WAS TALKING ABOUT NEEDING TO FIT INTO THE COMMUNITY?

COME ON.
I CAN'T BELIEVE YOU'RE MAKING ME DO THIS.

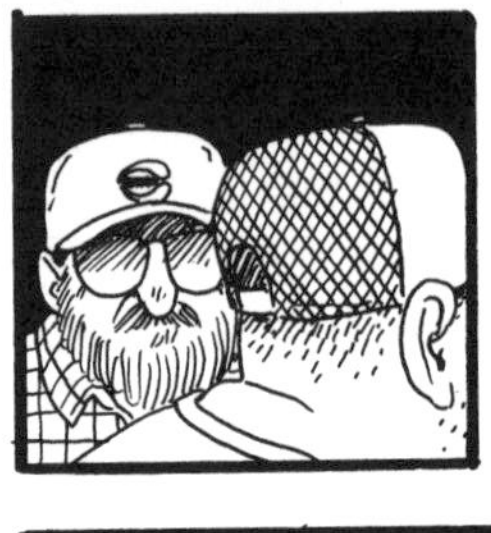

I WAS JUST TELLING ABE HERE ABOUT YOUR LITTLE FARMING OPERATION. HOW'S THE SEEDING GOING?

YOU SHOULD ASK MY SISTER. IT'S HER FARM.

FRIESEN'S FARMS, RIGHT?

HEY, WHAT DO YOU CALL A MENNONITE WHO FALLS THROUGH THE ICE?

DICK FRIESEN.

CLASSIC.
HAVEN'T HEARD THAT ONE BEFORE.

IKE OVER HERE WANTED ME TO CALL IT ZEPHYR FARMS HAHAHA

BUT SHE WAS CONVINCED WE'D DO BETTER IF WE FLEW THE MENNONITE FLAG.

WELL? WAS I WRONG?

AH, I SEE WE'VE GOT OURSELVES A REAL ENTREPRENEUR OVER HERE.

WE'RE MAKING PROGRESS. IT'S LOOKING TO BE A WET SPRING AND WE'VE BEEN HAVING DRAINAGE ISSUES, SO I'M TRYING TO FIGURE OUT HOW TO SOLVE THAT.

THERE'S AN OLD CREEK BED ON YOUR PROPERTY—GARY TRIED TO RECLAIM IT WHEN HE OWNED THE LAND.
NOT SURE THERE'S MUCH YOU CAN DO WITH IT.

I CAN BRING OVER MY CAT AND MOVE SOME SOIL AROUND FOR YOU.

WORTH A SHOT.

THAT'S MY CUE.

Thomas

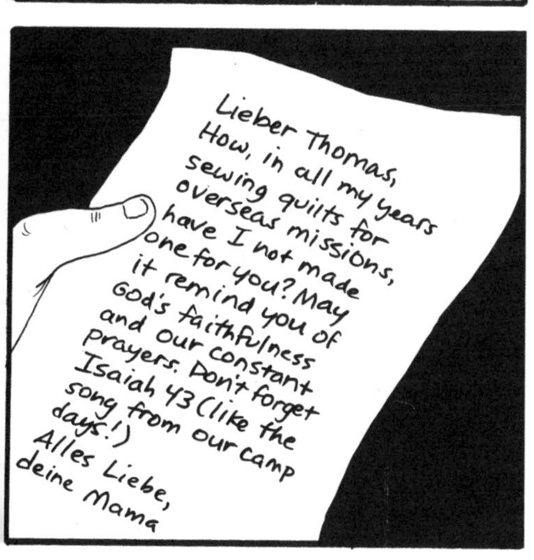
Lieber Thomas,
How, in all my years
sewing quilts for
overseas missions,
have I not made
one for you? May
it remind you of
God's faithfulness
and our constant
prayers. Don't forget
Isaiah 43 (like the
song from our camp
days!)
Alles Liebe,
deine Mama

FEAR NOT! FOR I HAVE REDEEMED YOU...

I HAVE CALLED YOU BY NAME AND YOU ARE MINE
CAMP

WITNESS

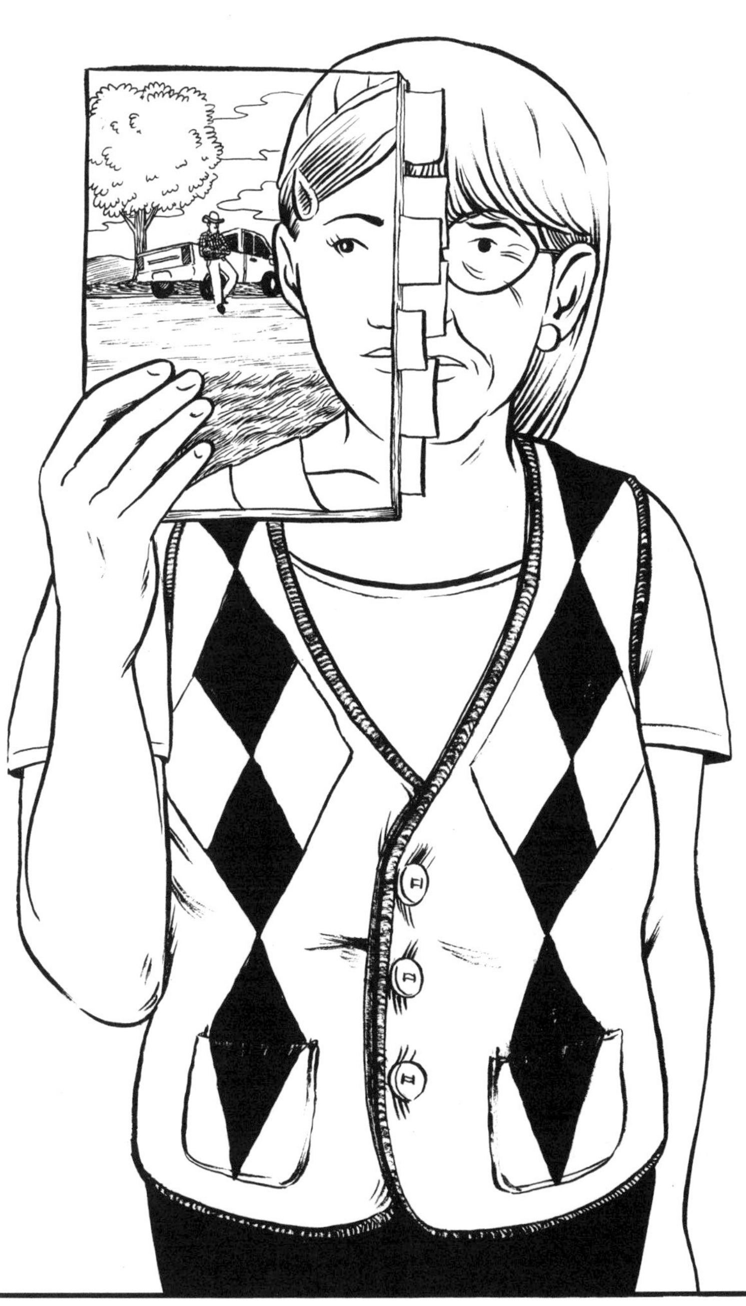

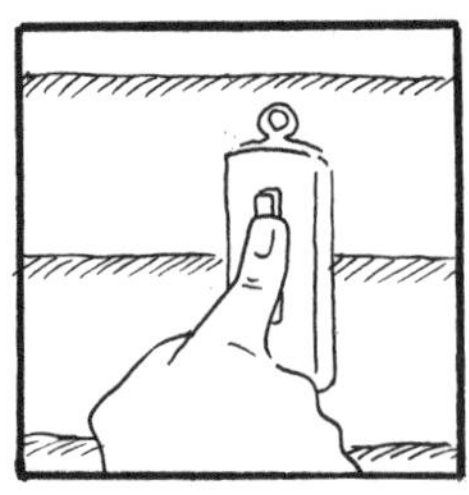

JUST A MINUTE!

HELLO
HI. HOW CAN I HELP YOU?

THIS IS FOR YOU.
Learn GOD'S PLAN FOR YOUR life

I'D LIKE TO INVITE YOU TO OUR CHURCH. WE HAVE TWO SERVICES EVERY SUNDAY. ONE AT 10:30 THE OTHER AT 4:30 IN THE AFTERNOON.

WE PROVIDE CHILD CARE AND HAVE SUNDAY SCHOOL FOR ALL AGE GROUPS. THERE'S ALSO A GROUP FOR SENIORS.

...I'VE ALREADY GOT A CHURCH I'VE BEEN ATTEND-ING FOR TWENTY YEARS.

BUT THANKS ANYWAY.

WAIT!
YES?

ARE YOU 100% SURE THAT YOU'LL GO TO HEAVEN WHEN YOU DIE?

NO.

BUT YOU SHOULDN'T BE SO SURE OF THAT EITHER.

IT SAYS IN THE BIBLE—
SLAM

THAT POOR WOMAN.

LIBRARY

DOING BOOK ORDERS?
YES, INDEED.

TRY NOT TO USE UP THE ENTIRE BUDGET ON CHRISTIAN FICTION THIS TIME, OK?

HAHA, UNFORTUNATELY I HAVE TO BUY BOOKS THAT WILL ACTUALLY GET TAKEN OUT AND READ.
IT'S A FINE BALANCE.

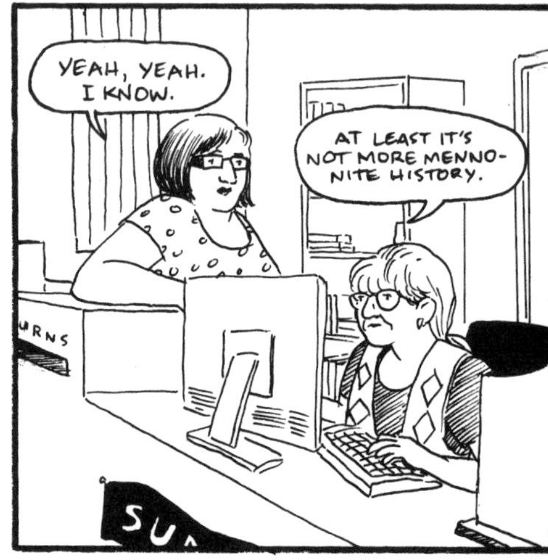
YEAH, YEAH. I KNOW.
AT LEAST IT'S NOT MORE MENNONITE HISTORY.

RETURNS
SUMMER READING

REMEMBER
RARY CARD?
Fields of Grace
FIELDS OF GRACE

THESE NEW BOOKS ARE READY TO BE SHELVED.

WANT ME TO PUT THEM OUT BEFORE THE END OF MY SHIFT?
YOU'VE ONLY GOT A FEW MINUTES LEFT. I'LL TAKE CARE OF THEM.

NEW
ARRIVALS

HI REBECCA-JUST WONDERING IF YOU WANTED TO COME OUT THIS WEEKEND AND HELP ME WITH A FEW BATCHES OF JAM.
SORRY. I'VE GOT A TERM PAPER TO FINISH, AND JASON IS GOING CAMPING.

ANOTHER TIME THEN.

YOU'LL NEVER GUESS WHO CAME BY THE HOUSE YESTERDAY.

THIS MOTHER AND DAUGHTER INVITED ME TO THEIR NEW CHURCH. AND WHEN I DECLINED THEY ASKED IF I KNEW WHETHER I WAS GOING TO HEAVEN.

IS IT THAT MASSIVE NEW CHURCH ON THE EDGE OF TOWN? WHAT'S IT CALLED AGAIN?
DO YOU MEAN PARK VALLEY?

NO, THEY WERE INVITING ME TO A DIFFERENT ONE — I THINK A SPLIT-OFF FROM ONE OF THE MORE CONSERVATIVE MENNONITE CHURCHES.
I WONDER WHAT IT'S OVER THIS TIME.

ANYWAY, THE WOMAN WHO CAME BY — I'M PRETTY SURE SHE VISITS THE LIBRARY.

I ALWAYS END UP FEELING SORRY FOR THE YOUNG WOMEN AT THOSE CHURCHES.
YEAH, IT CAN'T BE EASY.

IF YOU'RE SEEING HER AT THE LIBRARY, MAYBE YOU COULD SUGGEST SOME DIFFERENT READING MATERIAL TO HER, LIKE A STEPPING STONE.
YOU'RE IN THE PERFECT POSITION TO HELP.

I'M NOT SURE WHAT I'D BE HELPING WITH EXACTLY. I'D BE ASSUMING AN AWFUL LOT ABOUT HER SITUATION.
AND I ALREADY KIND OF TOLD HER OFF.

COME ON, MOM. WHAT IF YOU'RE HER ONLY CHANCE?

I'LL THINK ABOUT IT.

SO, WHEN ARE YOU COMING HOME NEXT?
ACTUALLY WE'RE GONNA BE PRETTY CLOSE TO YOU NEXT WEEKEND.

YOU KNOW THAT PIPELINE THAT RUNS THROUGH THE FARM? SOME INDIGENOUS LAND DEFENDERS HAVE SET UP A CAMP CLOSE TO THE BORDER, BLOCKING THE ROUTE.

YOU SHOULD MEET US THERE!
JASON SAID THEY'D WELCOME SUPPORT FROM PEOPLE WHO LIVE IN THE AREA.
I'LL SEND YOU DIRECTIONS.
OH, I DON'T THINK SO—I DOUBT I'LL BE OF MUCH HELP.
IT'S TIME FOR MY GENERATION TO STEP ASIDE. WE'VE MADE SUCH A MESS OF THINGS.
WHY DON'T YOU AND JASON COME OVER AFTERWARDS?
I'LL HAVE SOME SOUP AND BUNS READY.
YOU'RE ALWAYS SO FATALISTIC ABOUT THIS STUFF, MOM. WE ALL HAVE THINGS TO LEARN, WAYS TO CONTRIBUTE.
OF COURSE. AND I'M GLAD I CAN SUPPORT YOU.
SO MAYBE I'LL SEE YOU TWO FOR DINNER IN TWO WEEKS?
MAYBE.
SAY "HI" TO JASON FOR ME.

THRIFT SHOP
OPEN

CHANGE ROOMS

KITCHEN
FICTION
DVDs
CANNING SUPPLIES

LIDS

I'M NOT BUYING THESE FOR MY ENTERTAINMENT, YOU KNOW.

THE VOLUNTEERS HERE ARE TOO NAÏVE TO NOTICE WHAT KIND OF FILTH THEY'RE SELLING.

I COME ON THE DAYS THEY PUT OUT NEW ITEMS AND REMOVE THESE TEMPTATIONS.
THEN I BRING THEM STRAIGHT TO THE DUMP.

AND WHEN SOMETHING'S RIGHT ON THE EDGE OF BEING ACCEPTABLE, I WRITE DOWN A LITTLE NOTE AND SLIP IT INTO THE DVD CASE.

THAT'S VERY, UM, CONSIDERATE OF YOU.
IF YOU WANT TO FIND SOME REALLY SPICY STUFF YOU SHOULD TRY SIFTING THROUGH THE MENNONITE LITERATURE.

HEN
CHANGE ROOMS

HE HE HE.
PING!

KNOCK
KNOCK

OUR REAR ENDS BUMPED – HEHE. THERE DOESN'T APPEAR TO BE ANY DAMAGE, BUT MAYBE WE SHOULD TRADE INFORMATION, JUST IN CASE.

I WAS HERE FIRST. YOU SHOULD HAVE LOOKED WHERE YOU WERE GOING.
YES I'M SORRY BUT THERE ISN'T ANY DAMAGE THAT I CAN SEE.

THIS IS A BRAND NEW TRUCK. YOU NEED TO LEARN HOW TO DRIVE.
WAIT! DON'T I KNOW YOU FROM SOMEWHERE?

I HAVE NEVER SEEN YOU BEFORE.

AH, I KNOW! YOU'RE ONE OF THE MEN WHO'S ALWAYS PARKED BESIDE THE LIBRARY USING OUR WI-FI.

HAHA DON'T WORRY. I'M A LIBRARIAN SO I'M THERE, WELL, ALMOST EVERY DAY!

YOU CAN COME INSIDE, YOU KNOW — THE COMPUTERS, THE INTERNET, THE BOOKS — THEY'RE ALL FREE TO USE!

IT DOESN'T LOOK LIKE THERE'S ANY DAMAGE.

YOUR WIFE COMES IN. I'M SURE YOU SEE THE BOOKS SHE TAKES OUT.

WHEN ARE YOU TWO EXPECTING?

SLAM!

I'M SORRY. I SHOULDN'T HAVE SAID ANYTHING.

IT'S JUST THAT SHE WAS OVER AT MY HOUSE THE OTHER DAY TELLING ME ABOUT YOUR CHURCH – I WAS A BIT RUDE TO HER.

WAS THAT YOUNG GIRL WITH HER YOUR DAUGHTER?
T SHOP

THEY BOTH SEEMED VERY SWEET.
T SHO

HRIFT SHOP
WE'LL SEE YOU AT THE LIBRARY I HOPE!

NO FELIX!
OFF THE COUNTER!

Where calls the heart
NEW

CLICK

YOU'RE HERE EARLY. DON'T YOU WORK LATE TODAY?
JUST WANTED TO FINISH UP MY ORDERS. GOTTA GIVE THE PEOPLE WHAT THEY WANT.

I LOVE 2 READ
WORLD RECORDS

ESL

MORNING, KAREN.
HI ALF.

DO NOT TOUCH DIORAMA

FALLING UPWARD

FALLING UPW
BUZZ
BUZZ

SCHEISSE!

OH YOU DIDN'T MISS MUCH. ALF IS STILL IN THE HERITAGE ROOM AS PER USUAL.

I SHOULD GET AN EXTENDED LUNCH BREAK TOO.
OF COURSE - NO PROBLEM. HAVE A GOOD BREAK.

IT'S GONE!

OH KAREN, BY THE WAY COLIN WAS FILLING THE NEW ARRIVALS AND HE FOUND ONE OF OUR BOOKS FULL OF STICKY NOTES SITTING ON THE SHELF.
NEW ARRIVALS
I LOVE 2 READ

I DIDNT READ ALL OF THEM BUT IT'S CLEAR SOMEONE WANTED TO COMMUNICATE WITH WHOEVER WAS GOING TO READ THAT BOOK.
OH MY! REALLY?
I LOVE 2 READ

MOST OF THE NOTES WERE LEADING QUESTIONS ABOUT THE STORY - BUT THERE WERE ALSO COMMENTS LIKE "THINK FOR YOURSELF."
NEW ARRIVALS
AT LEAST THEY DIDN'T WRITE DIRECTLY IN THE BOOK.
AND I SAW THE WORD "PATRIARCHY" A FEW TIMES.

WE'LL HAVE TO BE ON THE LOOK OUT FOR THIS SORT OF THING.

FOR NOW, I'VE TOLD COLIN HE SHOULD JUST FLIP THROUGH THE BOOKS AS HE'S RESHELVING THEM.

SOME PEOPLE CAN'T HELP THEMSELVES. IT'S SAD HOW LITTLE WE TRUST EACH OTHER.

DING!
DING!

THAT'S QUITE A STACK YOU'VE GOT THERE!
YOU CAN BLAME ALF FOR THAT.

DOING SOME FAMILY RESEARCH?
BEEP
JUDITH SAWATZKY
Borrowed: 4
Hold: 2
Fees: 0.00

SORT OF... I NEEDED MORE CONTEXT. THERE ARE SO MANY MENNONITE GROUPS TO KEEP TRACK OF.

I KNOW JUST WHAT YOU MEAN. WHERE DO YOU EVEN START? RUSSIA? THE 1500s?
WELL, I'M TRYING TO START **HERE**.

...WITH THE PRIVILEGES MENNONITES GOT FROM THE GOVERNMENT ...AND THE TREATIES THAT ALLOWED US TO SETTLE HERE IN THE FIRST PLACE.

I JUST WISH THIS LIBRARY HAD MORE PERSPECTIVES FROM ... NON-MENNONITES.
WE'RE TRYING TO WORK ON THAT.
S
CLICK CLICK CLICK
CLICK CLICK CLICK
YAWN
CLICK
19 20 21
13 18 17 16 15
12 7 8 9 10
1 6 5 4 3
KNOCK KNOCK

HEY ALF, I'M CLOSING UP NOW. HOW DID OUR FAVOURITE HISTORIAN FARE TODAY?

PFFT! I AM AT BEST AN AMATUER.

THERE WERE SOME ARTEFACTS FOUND ON A BUILDING SITE LAST WEEK.

USED TO BE A FARMER'S FIELD.

APPARENTLY NOT IMPORTANT ENOUGH FOR MUSEUMS IN THE CITY TO CARE, BUT OUR TOWN HALL SAID THEY'D ADD THEM TO ONE OF THEIR DISPLAYS.

I'M SORTING OUT A TIMELINE OF LAND OWNERSHIP, SO THAT WE CAN NOTIFY THE FAMILY.

THERE ARE A NUMBER OF LEGERS, EACH WELL OVER A HUNDRED YEARS OLD, NICELY PRESERVED IN THE LOAM.

WHAT ARE THEY BUILDING THERE?
YOU KNOW THAT LARGE CHURCH ON THE SOUTH SIDE OF TOWN?

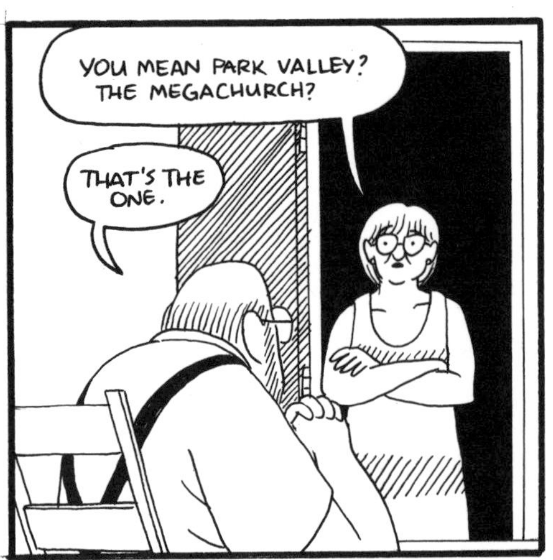
YOU MEAN PARK VALLEY? THE MEGACHURCH?
THAT'S THE ONE.

THEY'RE BUILDING AN EXPANSION WITH RECREATIONAL FACILITIES AND THE LIKE.

OH YES, I HEARD THERE'S EVEN A COFFEESHOP!
SHAMELESS!

AND THEN A BIT FURTHER SOUTH YOU HAVE THESE RIGID FUNDA-MENTALISTS LURING CONSERVATIVE MENNONITES TO ANOTHER NEW CHURCH.

TELLING THEM THEY'RE UNSAVED BECAUSE THEY DON'T HAVE THE CORRECT KIND OF BAPTISM.

IT'S NOT THEIR FIRST TIME TRYING TO PROSELYTIZE PEOPLE AROUND HERE, BUT THEY'VE NOW MANAGED TO PLANT A CHURCH.
SNAP

WE'RE LUCKY TO HAVE YOU HERE, ALF. HOW ELSE ARE WE GOING TO KEEP TRACK OF ALL THIS HISTORY?
I'M SIMPLY BEARING WITNESS.

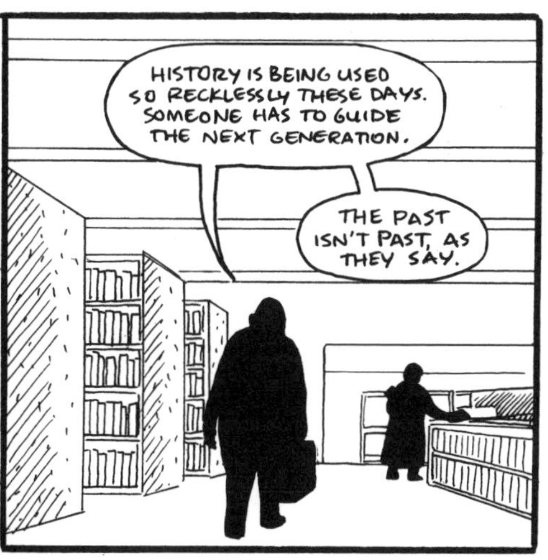
HISTORY IS BEING USED SO RECKLESSLY THESE DAYS. SOMEONE HAS TO GUIDE THE NEXT GENERATION.
THE PAST ISN'T PAST, AS THEY SAY.

AND MOST OF US ACT LIKE IT ONLY BEGAN WHEN OUR ANCESTORS GOT HERE.

INDEED, THIS PLACE WAS QUITE DIFFERENT BEFORE MEN-NONITES ARRIVED AND STARTED TO IMPROVE THE LAND.

"IMPROVE" FOR WHOM?
HM.?
SUMMER REA

FOR EVERYONE! WE TURNED THIS INTO SOME OF THE BEST FARMLAND IN THE WORLD!

THAT'S WHAT WE TELL OURSELVES.

DID YOU NEED A RIDE?
NO THANKS, ALF

I ALWAYS LOOK FORWARD TO THE WALK ON THESE WARM SUMMER NIGHTS.

POOL
POOL

VROOOM

MINNOWS

HURRY UP

THEY'RE PROBABLY THERE ALREADY.

I WISH THEY WOULD HAVE WAITED.

THEY KNEW WE'D BE A BIT LATE.

WE'RE THE ONES WHO HAD TO GO BUY GROCERIES.

WELL, I HOPE THEY LIKE VEGGIE DOGS. HA!

WE CAN TAKE OUR TIME, I GUESS.

YOU'RE PRETTY QUIET.

AREN'T YOU GONNA MISS DOING STUFF LIKE THIS?
YEAH, OF COURSE. BUT THE WEST COAST IS, LIKE, THIS TIMES A THOUSAND!

AND BEING OUT HERE ALWAYS REMINDS ME OF MY EVANGELICAL SUMMER CAMP.

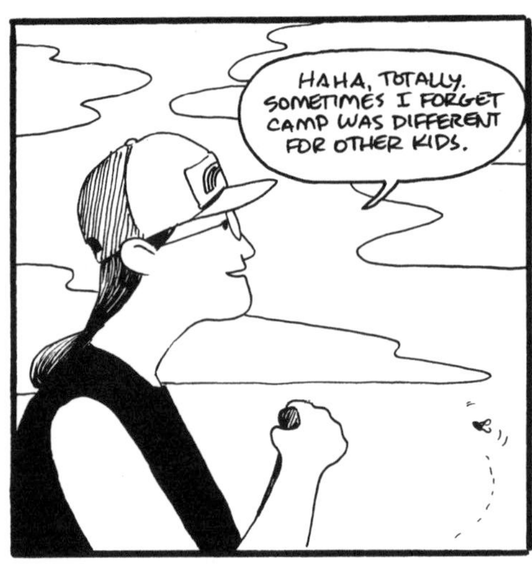
HAHA, TOTALLY. SOMETIMES I FORGET CAMP WAS DIFFERENT FOR OTHER KIDS.

I'M EXCITED TO VISIT YOU.

I HAVE SOME COUSINS CLOSE TO VANCOUVER.

IT'S TOO BAD REBECCA COULDN'T COME.

I GUESS THIS IS KIND OF OUR LAST HURRAH.

I'M GONNA STAY WITH JASON AND HER BEFORE I HEAD OUT.

I WISH WE COULD HAVE BEEN AT CAMP TOGETHER.

YOU COULD HAVE SEEN ME ON FIRE FOR THE LORD.

AT MY CAMP WE WERE ALL SUCH WEIRDOS, VERY DOWN WITH HIPPY JESUS.

I GUESS I WAS LUCKY.
HEY GUYS!

THANKS FOR WAITING!
ZIP

YEAH, SORRY ABOUT THAT.
WE THOUGHT WE COULD USE THE EXTRA TIME TO CATCH DINNER.

HOW'S REBECCA'S SUMMER COURSE GOING?
AMAZING
OKAY, I THINK. SHE REALLY WANTS TO GRADUATE THIS YEAR.

WELL TELL HER I MISS HER.
WHAT KIND OF FISH ARE THESE?

IT'S CALLED A CRAPPIE.

HAHA REALLY? NEVER HEARD OF IT.

WHAT ARE YOU DOING?
TAKE MY PICTURE!

IT'S ALL THAT'S MISSING FROM MY DATING PROFILE.
NONE OF THOSE GUYS ARE GOING TO REALIZE YOU'RE TROLLING THEM.
I LIKE TO KEEP THINGS SUBTLE.

HAHA! DON'T I KNOW IT!

PERFECT.

HEY! WE'VE GOTTA EAT THAT!
JESS, ARE YOU GETTING THIS?

JEEZ! LIGHTEN UP DEREK!

WHY DID JASON HAVE TO INVITE DEREK?
OH, HE'S NOT THAT BAD
AT LEAST THEY'RE THE ONES MAKING SUPPER.

FOOD'S READY.
GOOD DIVISION OF LABOUR, GUYS!

THANKS FOR GETTING MARSHMALLOWS.
NO PROB.

YOU BETTER EAT ALL THOSE.
SUSIE! YOUR MARSHMALLOWS ARE BURNING!

WAIT—WERE THOSE THE LAST ONES?!
SORRY.

HERE, YOU CAN HAVE MINE.

WHOA, THEY'RE PERFECTLY ROASTED.

YOU GUYS DON'T KNOW THIS BUT DEREK IS A FORMER McDON-ALDS GRILLMASTER.
HAHA SHUT UP, MAN.

I'M GLAD IT'S A CLEAR NIGHT. THE STARS ARE GONNA BE AMAZING.

DID YOU GUYS HAPPEN TO BRING ANY MUSHROOMS?
YEAH, I WAS THINKING TEA WOULD BE EASIEST.

SUCH A PRO.

THIS DOESN'T EVEN TASTE THAT BAD.

THE BUGS ARE OUT. I'M GOING TO GET MY JACKET.
CAN YOU GRAB MY SWEATER TOO?

SO DEREK—
HOW'S LARISSA?
I THINK I SAW
ON INSTAGRAM
THAT SHE JUST
GOT BACK
FROM A TRIP?

OH. YOU DON'T
KNOW? WE BROKE OFF
THE ENGAGEMENT
LIKE, A MONTH AGO.

SHIT... SORRY.
HOW ARE YOU
DOING?

IT'S BEEN
ROUGH, YOU
KNOW. WE WERE
TOGETHER A
LONG TIME.
PFFT

SHE STARTED GOING TO
THAT MEGACHURCH IN TOWN—
THEY BASICALLY TURNED
HER AGAINST ME.

WE WERE ARGUING
ABOUT IT ALL
THE TIME.
SCRATCH
SCRATCH
I STILL WORRY
ABOUT HER.

HM.

BUT DIDN'T YOU KIND OF ABANDON HER?

IT'S NOT LIKE I'M PROUD OF MYSELF.

HOW CAN I TRUST HER WITH A FAMILY, OR WITH MY MONEY?
WOW.

POINTS FOR HONESTY I GUESS.

SOUNDS LIKE IT WAS FOR THE BEST.

YEAH, YOU'RE PROBABLY RIGHT.

SHOULD WE PLAY A GAME?

ANYONE ELSE FEELING THE TEA?

THE STARS —THEY'RE DEFINITELY DOING STUFF.

SWIMMING AROUND THE SKY LIKE MINNOWS.

I'M TRYING TO FIND THE BIG DIPPER.
FOR SOME REASON IT'S HARDER THAN USUAL.

GEE. I WONDER WHY.
MAYBE ALIENS MOVED IT.

HONESTLY THAT UFO STUFF USED TO TERRIFY ME.

DID YOU GUYS EVER GO TO SUMMER CAMP WHEN YOU WERE KIDS?

NOPE
YEAH, A COUPLE TIMES.
JESS AND I WERE TALKING ABOUT IT ON THE WAY HERE.

ON THE LAST NIGHT OF CAMP WE'D ALWAYS SING AROUND THE CAMPFIRE, SHARE MEMORIES OR TEACHINGS FROM THE WEEK.

WE'D BE INVITED TO STAY BEHIND IF WE WANTED TO TALK TO A COUNSELLOR ONE-ON-ONE.

I REMEMBER THOSE.

THE SNEAKY ALTAR CALL.

WHAT'S AN ALTAR CALL?

IT'S, LIKE, THIS THING SOME CHURCHES DO AT THE END OF A SERVICE.
THEY'LL INVITE PEOPLE UP TO THE FRONT AND, YOU KNOW, GET THEM TO COMMIT THEMSELVES TO GOD.

ALL THOSE YEARS I WENT I ONLY EVER STAYED BEHIND ONCE. AND IT WAS BECAUSE I WANTED TO ASK WHETHER ALIENS EXIST.

WELL? WHAT KIND OF ANSWER DID YOU GET?
DID SHE TELL YOU THERE ARE UFOS IN THE BOOK OF EZEKIEL?

SHE SAID THAT IF THEY DID EXIST, WE DIDN'T NEED TO WORRY BECAUSE GOD CREATED THEM — OR SOMETHING LIKE THAT.

BY THAT POINT IN THE WEEK I WAS SO TERRIFIED OF GOING TO HELL I DIDN'T REALLY KNOW WHAT TO DO WITH THAT.

NO KIDDING.

ARE THOSE SUNFLOWER SEEDS?

MY OMA SAID SOMETHING SIMILAR TO ME ABOUT MONSTERS WHEN I WAS LITTLE, THAT WE DIDN'T NEED TO BE AFRAID.

PRETTY DEEP STUFF.
SUNNY DAY
SUNFLOWER SEEDS
SALTED

I DO FEEL LIKE I EXPERIENCED SOMETHING SPECIAL AT CAMP.

I MEAN, MAYBE IT WAS GOD, OR MAYBE IT WAS JUST NATURE.
WHO'S TO SAY.

JUST NATURE?

YOU KNOW THAT FOR MOST CULTURES IT'S NOT AN EITHER/OR.

YEAH, REMEMBER THAT BIBLE VERSE ABOUT HOW WE WERE GIVEN DOMINION OVER NATURE? THAT REALLY TURNED OUT WELL.

I DUNNO... I MEAN I KNOW LOTS OF PEOPLE THINK THAT LETS THEM OFF THE HOOK...

BUT AT THE CAMP I WENT TO ALL WE TALKED ABOUT WAS CREATION.

IT MADE ME FEEL SMALL... AND I KIND OF LIKED THAT.

THEN AGAIN - IT'S NOT LIKE WE EVER LEARNED ABOUT WHOSE LAND WE WERE ON.

I'M NOT SAYING IT CAN'T BE DIFFERENT.

BUT YOU STILL SEE THAT MINDSET EVERY-WHERE... NATURE IS EITHER A RESOURCE TO EXPLOIT OR IT'S AN ESCAPE.

THERE'S NO REASON **NOT** TO BELIEVE THAT OTHER LIFE EXISTS OUT THERE.

BUT, LIKE, SHOULDN'T WE BE MORE FOCUSSED ON SAVING THE PLACE WHERE WE ACTUALLY LIVE?

AND NOW WE HAVE ALL THESE IDIOTS WHO WANT TO COLONIZE OTHER PLANETS.

I THINK I JUST SAW A FISH JUMP!
SLAP!

SLAP!

UNNY DAY
SEEDS
SALTED

HEY DOES ANYBODY HAVE BUG SPRAY?

WHERE WE COME FROM IT'S PRETTY OBVIOUS RELIGION JUST MAKES PEOPLE DUMBER.

TOO BAD YOU CAN'T USE THAT EXCUSE.

CRACK
OUCH.

JESS - WHAT ARE YOU DOING?!

I-I HAVE TO MOVE AROUND!
I'M BEING EATEN ALIVE
THE BUGS!
SCRATCH
SLAP!
MAYBE A SHORT WALK.

DON'T GO TOO FAR. THE BUGS ARE DEFINITELY WORSE OUT THERE.

SHOULD WE GO WITH HER..?
NAH, SHE'LL BE FINE.

GOD, NATURE...
NATURE, GOD...

SCRATCH

GASP!

THANK YOU!

I USED TO
BE AFRAID
OF YOU

AFRAID OF MYSELF.

WHAT DO YOU SEE?

DO YOU EVER LOOK AT THE STARS?

DO YOU KNOW THAT THE WORLD IS BURNING?

OF COURSE YOU DO...

AAAAAARRGHH
OH SHIT.

WE'RE COMING, JESS!
I'LL GRAB A FLASH-LIGHT.

OH. HEY GUYS.

LET'S BRING HER BACK TO THE FIRE. I HAVE A FIRST AID KIT.
OUCH!

I LOVE YOU GUYS.
LOOKS LIKE IT'S JUST A BAD SCRAPE. HOPEFULLY WE STILL HAVE SOME ICE.
EVEN YOU, DEREK.
THANKS

JESS, CAN YOU HOLD STILL?
I THINK I GET IT NOW.

OH YOU DO, DO YOU?
WE'RE ALL CONNECTED.

HAHA SURE.
HERE'S AN ICE PACK.

LET'S GET YOU TO BED, JESS.
YA, THAT'S PROBABLY BEST.

WELL, I'M GLAD THE MUSHROOMS ARE WORKING FOR YOU.
I LOVE YOU, SUSIE.

LOVE YOU TOO, JESS. DO YOU NEED ANYTHING ELSE?
ZIIIIP
I'LL BE FINE.

TOOT!

OOOEHEOOOOOO...

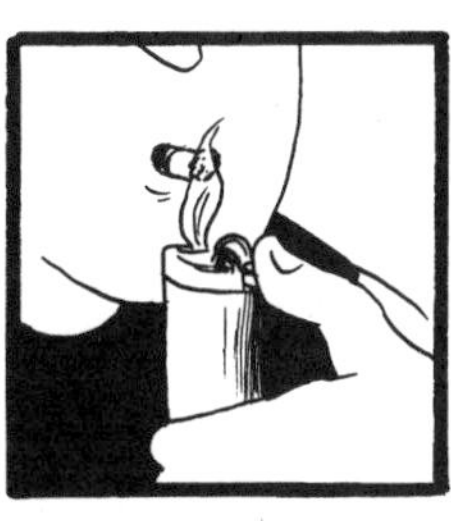

CAN I GET ONE OF THOSE?

HOW'S THE ARM?

A LITTLE SORE BUT NOT TOO BAD.

SORRY IF I GOT A BIT OUT OF HAND LAST NIGHT. WHAT TIME DID YOU GUYS END UP GOING TO BED?

I WENT JUST AS THE SUN STARTED COMING UP - NOT SURE ABOUT SUSIE AND DEREK.

I GET THAT DEREK IS REBECCA'S COUSIN BUT I DON'T KNOW HOW YOU BOTH STAND HIM.
I KNOW IT'S WEIRD THAT I BROUGHT HIM, BUT HE'S BEEN PRETTY DOWN SINCE THE BREAK UP AND WE NEEDED TO FILL REBECCA'S SPOT.

JUST SO YOU KNOW, I SAW THAT SUSIE'S TENT WAS LEFT OPEN THIS MORNING, SO I THINK THEY'RE, UM—
YOU'RE JOKING

THAT'S A MEAN JOKE.

YOU DIDN'T HEAR IT FROM ME, OK?

I THOUGHT I SHOULD WARN YOU. I KNOW THERE'S —
STOP, PLEASE!

SORRY JESS —I THOUGHT YOU'D WANT TO KNOW.

SNUFFLE

ZIP
FUCK

JESS!

HOLD UP.
DON'T TOUCH ME.

YOUR ARM!

I BROUGHT YOU SOME COFFEE AND PANCAKES.

I'M HERE IF YOU WANT TO TALK.
I'M GONNA TRY AND FINISH MY BOOK.

I'M REALLY SORRY ABOUT YOUR ARM.
DEREK IS A MORON.

YEAH, I'M AWARE OF THAT.

IT'S JUST HARD FOR ME TO SEE YOU GO.

THEN WHY WON'T YOU COME WITH ME?

YOU'RE GONNA GET STUCK IN HESPELER AND THERE'S, LIKE, ZERO QUEER PEOPLE THERE.

THAT'S NOT TRUE.

I KNOW THERE ARE LOTS OF GOOD REASONS TO LEAVE

BUT I FEEL LIKE I'M JUST STARTING TO GET TO KNOW THIS PLACE.

WHERE ARE DEREK AND SUSIE?
THEY WENT FISHING.
I'M ABOUT TO GO FIND SOME BIRDS IF YOU WANT TO JOIN ME.
NAH, YOU GO AHEAD. I'VE GOT MY NOVEL TO READ.
OH COME, ON— YOU COULD DO THAT ANYWHERE.
SO, WHAT ARE YOU READING?

GIOVANNI'S ROOM.
I LOVE JAMES BALDWIN! RE-BECCA GOT ME TO READ THE FIRE NEXT TIME AND IT WAS AMAZING.

COOL - I'LL SEE IF THEY HAVE IT AT THE LIBRARY

HAHA - THERE'S NO WAY YOUR TOWN'S LIBRARY HAS THAT... I GUESS YOU COULD ASK REBECCA'S MOM.

HERE'S SOMETHING I BET YOU HAVEN'T SEEN BEFORE.
WHAT?

THERE'S A DOUBLE CRESTED CORMORANT NEST, JUST BEYOND THE SPRUCE IN FRONT OF US, NEAR THE TOP OF THAT DEAD POPLAR.

LOOKS LIKE THE MOTHER JUST CAME BACK FROM A HUNT.

SHE'S DRYING OFF IN THE SUN.

I CAN'T FIND IT.
TRY TO FOCUS ON THE TREE WITHOUT THE BINOCULARS AND THEN RAISE THEM TO YOUR EYES.
I-I CAN SEE THEM.
DO YOU THINK SHE CAN SEE US?
THE MOTHER? SHE SPOTTED US BEFORE WE EVEN GOT HERE.

SHOULD WE KEEP GOING?

DEFINITELY.

SLUUURP

Sept. 25
Serve
summer CAMP

PLAZA
SALE

BIBLE MENNONITE FELLOWSHIP

PARK VALLEY CHURCH
COME COOL OFF WITH AN ICED LATTE AT OUR NEW CAFE!

FRIESEN'S farms
OPEN

PROTECT THE SACRED
NO

NOTES

THE EPIGRAPH IS TAKEN FROM THE ESSAY "FIELD" BY JOHN BERGER. *THE SENSE OF SIGHT: SELECTED ESSAYS*. NEW YORK: VINTAGE, 1993.

p. 47 - LYRICS FROM "BOMBS" BY BUCKY DRIEDGER. USED WITH PERMISSION.

p. 81 - PATCH FEATURES "THUNDERBIRD WOMAN" ARTWORK BY ISAAC MURDOCH. USED WITH PERMISSION.

p. 82 - LYRICS FROM "MY FAVOURITE CHORDS" BY JOHN K. SAMSON ON *LEFT AND LEAVING* BY THE WEAKERTHANS. EPITAPH RECORDS, 2000. USED WITH PERMISSION.

AN EXCERPT FROM AN EARLIER VERSION OF "BETTER TIMES" (pp 136-152) APPEARED IN *HAMILTON ARTS & LETTERS* 13.2, 2020-21.

AN EXCERPT FROM AN EARLIER VERSION OF "MINNOWS" (pp 213-243) APPEARED IN *BROADVIEW* MAGAZINE. OCTOBER, 2020.

THANK YOU

I'M GRATEFUL TO EVERYONE WHO READ EARLIER VERSIONS OF THESE STORIES AND SHARED THEIR IMPRESSIONS WITH ME: JOSIAH NEUFELD, CASEY PLETT, WARREN CARIOU, CAM SCOTT, ANDREW LOEWEN, JOHN K. SAMSON, DAVID DRIEDGER, TANYA SUDERMAN, SUE SORENSEN, JONI SAWATZKY AND Q. A. C.

THANK YOU SARAH ENS FOR EDITING THAT WENT ABOVE AND BEYOND.

THANK YOU TO THE MANITOBA ARTS COUNCIL FOR SUPPORTING THIS PROJECT AND THANKS TO PLUG-IN ICA'S SHOP FOR THEIR HELP SELLING MY POSTERS AND SELF-PUBLISHED COMICS WHEN SHELTERBELTS WAS JUST GETTING OFF THE GROUND.

THANK YOU ANDY BROWN AND EVERYONE AT CONUNDRUM PRESS.

AND THANKS MOST OF ALL TO MY PARENTS WHO KEEP ME COMING BACK.

— JD, 2022
TREATY ONE TERRITORY AND HOMELAND OF THE MÉTIS.